Labyrinths
from the
Outside In

SECOND EDITION

Walking to Spiritual Insight
A BEGINNER'S GUIDE

REV. DR. DONNA SCHAPER
REV. DR. CAROLE ANN CAMP

Walking Together, Finding the Way®
SKYLIGHT PATHS®
PUBLISHING
Woodstock, Vermont

Labyrinths from the Outside In, 2nd Edition:
Walking to Spiritual Insight—a Beginner's Guide

2013 Quality Paperback Edition, First Printing
© 2013, 2000 by Donna Schaper and Carole Ann Camp

For information regarding permission to reprint material from this book, please mail or fax your request in writing to SkyLight Paths Publishing, Permissions Department, at the address / fax number listed below, or e-mail your request to permissions@skylightpaths.com.

Library of Congress Cataloging-in-Publication Data

Schaper, Donna.
 Labyrinths from the outside in : walking to spiritual insight : a beginner's guide / Rev. Donna Schaper & Rev. Carole Ann Camp. — 2nd [edition].
     pages cm
 "Walking Together, Finding the Way."
 Includes bibliographical references.
 ISBN 978-1-59473-486-1
 1. Labyrinths—Religious aspects. 2. Spiritual life. I. Camp, Carole Ann. II. Title.
 BL325.L3S33 2013
 203'.7—dc23

                                   2013005410

10 9 8 7 6 5 4 3 2 1

Manufactured in the United States of America
Cover Art: © shutterstock.com/col
Cover Design: Heather Pelham

SkyLight Paths Publishing is creating a place where people of different spiritual traditions come together for challenge and inspiration, a place where we can help each other understand the mystery that lies at the heart of our existence.

SkyLight Paths sees both believers and seekers as a community that increasingly transcends traditional boundaries of religion and denomination—people wanting to learn from each other, *walking together, finding the way.*

Skylight Paths, "Walking Together, Finding the Way," and colophon are trademarks of LongHill Partners, Inc., registered in the U.S. Patent and Trademark Office.

Walking Together, Finding the Way®
Published by SkyLight Paths Publishing
A Division of LongHill Partners, Inc.
Sunset Farm Offices, Route 4, P.O. Box 237
Woodstock, VT 05091
Tel: (802) 457-4000   Fax: (802) 457-4004
www.skylightpaths.com

Contents

Preface to the Second Edition
   Walking a Labyrinth: Another Kind of Power   vii

Introduction
   Labyrinths from the Outside In   1

Part One
Approaching the Labyrinth
DONNA SCHAPER

1. The Labyrinth Revival   17

2. The Absolute Meets the Ancient:
    What Labyrinths Do   29

3. What Is Spiritual about the Labyrinth?   39

4. Spiritual Authority in the Labyrinth   49

Part Two
Walking the Labyrinth
CAROLE ANN CAMP

5. Hearing the Dark: Elements of the Labyrinth Walk   61

6. Walks for Rites of Passage   79

7. Walks for the Four Seasons   97

8. Walking in Many Spiritual Traditions   109

9. Walks for the Celtic Year and the Zodiac   127

Epilogue: Labyrinths from the Inside Out   145

Appendix A: Making Your Own Labyrinth   151

Appendix B: Finding a Labyrinth in Your Area   164

Notes   189

Photo Credits   190

Walking a canvas labyrinth outdoors.

Preface to the Second Edition

WALKING A LABYRINTH: ANOTHER KIND OF POWER

MANY OF US LIVE LIFE WALKING IN CIRCLES WITHOUT much intention. We feel a little caught, trapped, encumbered: we make our next move because somebody else or some other thing made its move. We get "tied up in knots;" life feels tangled and twisted. We don't move so much as feel moved upon.

Walking a labyrinth is different. Here we walk in a circle with much intention. We let the circle guide us as we guide our feet. We un-knot. We untangle. We twist and turn toward peace, away from powerlessness.

Walking a labyrinth is neither passive nor active but both, mixed with an intention. Its intention is to acknowledge the circle. We let the circle guide us; that is the passive part. We guide the circle; that is the active part. Instead of having someone put the moves on us, we move, while understanding that we are also moved upon by the great circle of life. We see the circling, from birth through death, from morning through evening, from winter through spring and back again, as the template for our days.

Having the moves put on us can be fun, or affirming— someone is flirting with us. But even in the best romances, we need to remain ourselves. We need to guide our own feet and not let them be guided by others, even the best of others, even our mother, father, sister, brother, or lover. A labyrinth walk, simple but powerful, puts us in a community driver's seat: we let others have action in our lives even as we maintain the action of our own moves. We see our own selves as a whole, active passives or passive actives. We live a great attached detachment.

Since the first edition of this book was published in 2000, the use of labyrinths as spiritual practice has exploded. They are found in small and large towns, at cathedrals and country churches, in prisons and malls. Once something that needed explanation, now labyrinths are common, part of our folk knowledge.

Many people use the labyrinth spiritually, as a way of entering the circle of life with great intention. We walk one on our birthdays or anniversaries or after a loved one has died. We also walk the great circle just for the sake of walking it, when we want to become new or different or feel a little less encumbered by the demands of life.

More and more people are walking the labyrinth because it helps them manage the great circling of life. Circling is the spiritual acknowledgment of life's ups and downs, ins and outs—and how we often have to leave home to get home. Home is always the destination but it is rarely easy, except for those who are in denial of life's dangers and dramas.

On the second night of Hurricane Sandy in New York City, we put out our canvas labyrinth in the sanctuary. We didn't know what else to do, as we were in the deep dark of lost electrical power. We also knew that scant miles away many people had lost everything to the powerful storm.

That night about twenty of us gathered, along with one dog, to walk the circle, light candles, sing a few songs and say a few prayers. The giant canvas labyrinth was easy to put out in the dark, with its white stripes.

As we walked its path, we observed what our hearts know: there are many different kinds of power. Too many people were saying they were "out of power," or "powerless." More precisely, we were without electrical power. We still had the power to circle and to gather.

So we walked our labyrinth. We had to remind ourselves that there are different kinds of power than the kind we didn't have. There is people power, candlepower, physical power (you couldn't volunteer for the Red Cross if you couldn't lift fifty pounds or stay for twelve hours), magical power, the power that makes you think the A train will be humming again soon. There is the power to hear words anew: *infrastructure*, *nature*, *air*, *wind*, *fire*. There is the power to recognize, as the labyrinth shows, that in every end there is a beginning. New York will never be the same. We know that. Jones Beach is mostly gone, as are the Rockaways. What is not gone is the great circle of life.

What is new in the ancient practice of labyrinth walking is that it has "come back." It might have been there all along, even though we didn't know we were walking labyrinths all the time. Perhaps we were just walking intentionally. Or walking in circles. Or meditating while walking or walking while meditating. Perhaps we were letting our feet do the praying as we emptied our minds of heaviness and leaned into lightness.

What is new in the ancient practice is that, once again, we have a name for it. We almost whisper it. *I'm walking the labyrinth*, we'll say, and instead of having to explain ourselves, people know what we mean. They have seen a labyrinth at a church or hospital or community center or town park or flower store or mall. They have met someone who counseled them to try walking a labyrinth to alleviate stress or to make a decision.

We wish we could count how many more labyrinths there are now than when we did our first edition, but there are so many that we couldn't possibly aim for accuracy. We can assuredly say that the comeback of the ancient walking is real and pervasive. People may remain mystified or quizzical but they know that labyrinths are something people did of yore and now do again. The practice, once so dusty, has now become very popular.

Perhaps the reason is the increased stress in our world—and the fact that many mental health professionals advise meditation as well as medication. Or it may be the return of respect for folk cultures, that nagging sense many of us have that the enlightenment stole something from us. Or just the sense many of us have that we need to be more *physical* in our spirituality. Like yoga, labyrinth walking lets you do material things in a spiritual way. Surely the comeback of labyrinths is also rooted in the reasonable suspicion many of us have of the rational unconnected to the spiritual or the communal or the ancient. We wonder why the soul became so isolated from our daily lives. Labyrinth walking returns us to matters of the soul, the rational-plus, the calm of repose, all of which more and more people are willing to admit they need.

Whatever the reason for the labyrinth's return, it is back. We are thrilled to release this new edition as a way to support a growing spiritual practice in a world groaning for ways to be more peaceful, more calm, more spirit filled. In this edition we've updated our labyrinth listings for the United States and added listings for Canada. You'll also find new listings for memorial labyrinths and hospital, university, and retreat center labyrinths in addition to those at churches. We hope you'll make full use of these resources to experience the variety of labyrinths that have sprung up in the last decade.

Labyrinth walking is a ritual remembrance of what we already know. Before Hurricane Sandy, we had known for a long time about climate change and aging infrastructure. Now we *know* that we know, and we have a different kind of power—the kind that moves people to change. We circle into reality actively, with an intention to understand, and passively, because a big storm (or just life) put the moves on us.

Labyrinth walking also helps us name our joy out loud. A pregnant woman walks a labyrinth to welcome the new baby that will change her understanding of home forever. A divorced man walks to the edges of the circle, knowing that his home is now different, as different as he is. A college graduate walks the circle in order to enjoy her commencement. A lover dies, and we walk the labyrinth to let what we know sink in. And sometimes we just walk the labyrinth to notice that we are alive and changing. Perhaps we have aged and were unaware. Or lost more hope than we thought we had lost. Or realize we like our current job. Whatever the change—and there is always change, with or without a big storm to announce it—we walk for awareness of how we have been acted upon and how we may yet act.

The labyrinth is finally just a circle, usually made of physical materials like stones or canvas, bricks or poured concrete. Sometimes they are just chalked on a sidewalk. But this circle is a spiritual one—and its power is accessible by anybody who wants to come in.

A new labyrinth under construction.

Introduction

LABYRINTHS FROM THE OUTSIDE IN

LABYRINTHS ARE SPRINGING UP EVERYWHERE THESE days, in likely places such as gardens and parks and in unlikely places such as the middle of a New York City street, nursing homes, and veterans' hospitals. Their circularity challenges the millennial anxiety about where we are heading. Today's spiritual seekers want something for the new age that is ancient and substantial, not just "New Age." The labyrinth appeals to seekers of every faith and seekers with no or very little faith background.

The labyrinth has been used for centuries as a pilgrimage, a way back home. When Christian pilgrims could not get to Jerusalem, they walked the labyrinth. If we cannot solve today's problems, at least we can walk in a way and with a posture that says we are not mired in the problems. We still hope for ways out. The ways out are less anti-knot than they are knotted. We learn that inside the labyrinth. There, we do not deny complexity; rather, we walk it. Knots and webs and conundrums are the message of the labyrinth. We love them as they are, and we love them for what they represent. We are free to be with them; they pattern our lives toward home.

People often confuse labyrinths with mazes. In some ways labyrinths are like mazes, but a labyrinth is more than a maze. In a labyrinth you are never lost; you are always on the path leading into or back out of the center. One finds the center if one walks the path. A labyrinth is like a maze with a certain answer. It is maze-*plus*—once you know the labyrinth, you know there is a way into the center. Mazes remain puzzles because they can perplex permanently. Labyrinths are designed with the eventual solution fully on display: if we but walk the path, we get home.

A Bit of History

The labyrinth's origins as a spiritual homing device are lost in prehistory. Scholars offer contradictory evidence. But regardless, it is a fact that people from both ancient and modern cultures around the world and throughout time have looked to the labyrinth as an archetypal symbol of journey and spiritual renewal.

Some archaeologists and historians believe that the first labyrinths were in Egypt and Ertruria (now central Italy) around 4500 BCE. There is evidence that they were built at entrances of tombs to keep them inviolate. Evil spirits apparently did not like the planned order of the labyrinthian pattern. Nothing of these early labyrinths survives. The archaeologist Marija Gimbutas found a meandering labyrinthian pattern on a figurine from the Ukraine dated at 15,000 to 18,000 BCE and concluded that the labyrinth-like pattern may have predated the labyrinth itself.

Many of the buildings called labyrinths in antiquity consisted of subterranean passages with many rooms. About 2000 BCE, a building in northern Egypt, just east of the Lake of Moeris, was said to be a labyrinth. Herodotus (484–425 BCE), the first Greek historian of the ancient world and author of *The History of the Greco-Persian War*, visited this building and writes about it as a grave guarder. Although Herodotus refers to this building as a labyrinth, it is not like our present-day labyrinths. Herodotus reports that the Egyptian labyrinth had three thousand chambers and twelve courts. Imagining how something this big could be labyrinthian in shape is something we have to do without benefit of photographs or other pictures.

The origin of the word *labyrinth* is not universally agreed upon either. Some think that the word comes from *labrys*, the sacred double-headed ax associated with the Minoan palace of Knossos on the eastern Mediterranean island of Crete. The legend says that King Minos had Daedalus build a labyrinth, a house of winding passages, to house the bull-man, the Minotaur, the beast that his queen, Pasiphae, bore after having intercourse with a bull. (Hybrid animal-human creatures are often associated with the early labyrinth.) Minos had refused to sacrifice a bull to Poseidon as he had promised, so Poseidon took revenge by causing the queen to desire the bull. Minos then required tribute from Athens in the form of young men and women to be sacrificed to the Minotaur. Theseus, an Athenian, accompanied one of these groups of victims to the court of Minos, where Minos's daughter Ariadne fell in love with him. She gave him one end of a long thread to take with him into the labyrinth so that he was able to kill the Minotaur and then find his way out again. This Cretan labyrinth was actually a maze rather than what we now call a labyrinth. Some scholars contend that this labyrinth of King Minos existed only in myth. Whether real or fictitious, this legend has come to symbolize a death and rebirth ritual, a kind of heroic or initiatory rite.

In other parts of the world, there is evidence of people's connectedness to labyrinths, or at least to labyrinthian designs. The Nazcan civilization of about 500 BCE in southwestern Peru constructed a number of labyrinth-like figures on the Pampa del Ingenio, an extremely dry, flat desert. Some of these figures of spiders and spirals range in size from 46 meters to more than 285 meters. Colorful pottery found in the area and attributed to the Nazcan civilization often depicts labyrinths. The Hopi Indians of North America used a symbol known today as the "seven-path labyrinth." There is also evidence of crude stone labyrinths on the coasts of the Baltic and White Seas, designed and built by early Lapps.

It is believed that fishermen in Sweden, Finland, and Estonia built labyrinths and walked them before going out to sea to ensure a good wind and a good catch. The fishermen would walk into the labyrinth slowly, presumably with trolls, who represented ill-fated intentions, following them. Then they would run out of the labyrinths quickly and jump in their boats, leaving the slow-thinking trolls behind, stuck in the labyrinth.

During the early Middle Ages, European writers romanticized the story of the Trojan War, reworking the epic in their own medieval style. During this same period, many towns in northern Europe created labyrinths of various shapes, sizes, and styles in their towns. The builders of these labyrinths named them after the events in Troy. The reasoning behind their choice is something of a mystery, but the evidence is striking. In England, for example, there were labyrinths called Troy-towns, Walls of Troy, Caerdronia (a Welsh word meaning "Troy"), and Troja, Trojborg, or Troborg in Sweden.

Many of the Christian labyrinths appeared relatively late in history, also around the twelfth century, although the first

Plan of the turf labyrinth called Troytown, Somerton,
Oxfordshire, England.

Labyrinth of the Church of Reparatus, Orleansville, Algeria,
circa fourth century.

known labyrinth in a Christian church may be in the Church of Reparatus, Algeria, around the fourth century. When Christians could no longer make physical pilgrimages to their spiritual home in Jerusalem, they walked a symbolic pilgrimage on a labyrinth built into the floor of the nave of a cathedral. They turned a physical journey into a spiritual journey. If they could not get to Jerusalem, they made believe they were walking to Jerusalem on the labyrinth. Going into the labyrinth also symbolized a trip to the underworld, and the trip out was a resurrection; heaven and hell are both invoked in its pattern. Many of the churches containing labyrinths in France and Italy built during the early Middle Ages have been destroyed, although some have survived. The labyrinth in the cathedral in Rheims, France, built in 1240, was made of blue stones. The children walking the stone path made so much noise that the labyrinth was ordered destroyed in 1779. The cathedral in Amiens, France, which also contained a labyrinth, was built in 1288 and destroyed in 1825.

One of the most famous Christian labyrinths, and one that has survived intact, is found on the floor of the Chartres cathedral in France. The paving stones that make up the illustrious labyrinth trace a pattern that spans the entire width of the nave. Those who know of its existence and its history can find it hidden under the wooden chairs that litter it. The circle on the floor repeats the pattern of the stained-glass circle of the western rose window. This sort of architectural analogy of the medieval builders was essential to the thinking of the mathematicians and mystics who made up the school of Chartres. In the view of these Platonic philosophers, whatever existed on earth could be only a dim reflection of a higher reality that existed on another plane, but the reflection had to remain true to the original in number and proportion. People were going to a real city called Jerusalem, in a faux

Labyrinth of Amiens Cathedral, France.

Labyrinth of Chartres Cathedral, France.

pilgrimage, but they were also imitating a journey, which was understood as eternal and celestial.

Almost any labyrinth, like the one at Chartres, takes on the burden of representing other labyrinths while making its own particular spiritual statement. For example, from early on Christians thought the labyrinth represented the soul's journey to Christ. The whole cathedral at Chartres is a hymn of praise to the Christ. The rose window, its jewel, symbolizes heaven, with Christ at its center surrounded by four rings with twelve circles in each. Twelve is the number of the apostles. When this heavenly rose, which is composed of nothing but colored light, casts its image down to earth, it is transformed into a maze, a place of confusion and suffering for a pilgrim.

In many of the medieval church labyrinth patterns, there is a curious juxtaposition of Christian and non-Christian symbolism. In the church of San Savino at Piacenza, Italy (built 903–1107 CE), for example, the twelve signs of the zodiac encircle the labyrinth. The central stone at the Chartres labyrinth used to bear the following legend: "This stone represents the Cretan's labyrinth. Those who enter cannot leave unless they be helped, like Theseus, by Ariadne's thread."

Christian penitents wound their way on their knees to the center of the labyrinth and out again. The center was variously known as Jerusalem or heaven. At Chartres, there is a unique mix of maze and labyrinth, confusion and centeredness, Christian and pre-Christian. In the cruciform cathedrals of Chartres, Amiens, and Rheims, the labyrinth is in the same place, in the nave. If one sees the design of the building as representing the figure of Christ on the cross, this would put the labyrinth approximately at his knees.

Mystic connections surround the number 666: the Chartres cathedral used Aphrodite's six-lobed symbol in its center, mimicking the number of the beast in Revelation 13:18. These medieval Christians were borrowing from the Greeks, who might have borrowed from the Egyptians. No one can claim to know, but we can at least walk the labyrinth back to what might have been the beginning. We can imagine what might be way back there.

Not all labyrinths are the same, as though issued from some central certifying office. The classic seven-circuit labyrinth, for example, has been richly modified by many ancient cultures. They take many shapes and forms. They are as different as the cultures that created them and as wide ranging as the early artists who drew them from some place inside themselves and their picture of the world.

Early labyrinths are found not only in church naves and palace gardens but in many ordinary towns as well. The town of Saffron Walden, England, has a labyrinth with a single brick path that first appears in records in 1699, according to the accounts of the Guild of the Holy Trinity, who "paid 15 shillings for cutting the maze." The Saffron Walden labyrinth resembles the shape of the labyrinth at Rheims Cathedral. Other labyrinths in England, many made of turf, encompassed a variety of shapes and sizes.

Different times and different cultures have attributed and continue to attribute a variety of metaphorical meanings to the labyrinth. In ancient Irish and English legends, fairies danced on labyrinth spirals in the moonlight. In Norwegian and Swedish folktales, ice giants created stone labyrinths. In other legends, labyrinths mark the entrances and doorways to underground palaces.

An idea that spirals in and out of many local legends is that labyrinths represent uterine energy. This comes from the fact that ancients thought that the intestine was the uterus, or womb. In Kundalini yoga, the body is sometimes moved in a pattern that can be seen to imitate the labyrinth in miniature fashion. This movement meditation, called *yantra*, was used as a meditation by Hindu midwives to assist in childbirth

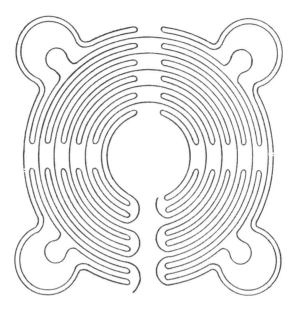

*Plan of the turf labyrinth of Saffron Walden,
Essex, England.*

*Reconstructed plan of the labyrinth of Poitiers
Cathedral, France.*

and as a means of relaxation for the birth canal—again, improperly imagined as intestinal. The postures are called *gateways* and remind us of the way that many ancient peoples used labyrinths as sacred gateways, posting them not only on doorposts or graves but also at the entrances to cities and towns. They were located at the points that people thought contained subtle earth energies.

The symbolic return to the womb before sacramental rebirth is a part of many ancient religions: one travels the cord backward in order to go forward. Christians symbolically "drown" initiates during baptism as a way of symbolizing the death that will come and the death that preceded birth. The umbilical cord is related to the symbols of thread and cord, which also weave in and out of the labyrinth myths and stories.

In Hindu and Buddhist art we also find combinations of sacred bulls, umbilical cords, and labyrinths, usually with a bull mask called Yama. In other eastern fables, this bull becomes a minotaur, just as with the Greeks. In all these faiths, a similar biological mistake grounded the labyrinth—the belief that the intestines and uterus were connected—with the result that the intestines were used as a model for the labyrinth. In all the myths, a connection is made between birth and death: life's circle is from womb to tomb, from an original darkness to a new kind of darkness. If labyrinths do nothing else, they offer symmetry and connection as a picture of life as it really is. The spiral represents the generation of energy. When its coil is unwound, stored energy is released.

Inner understandings—whether biologically correct or not—shape outer understandings. From ancient times, the labyrinth was associated with pilgrimage routes and rituals of self-discovery. Labyrinths serve as time windows or portals where time stands still so that we can remember what we are doing. Labyrinths are a part of the culture and ritual that tells us who we are, as Emile Durkheim, the French sociologist, asserted. Many ancient peoples related the labyrinth to childbirth in various ways. The labyrinth of Crete contained 272 stones—the same as the average number of days in the human gestation period.

Getting out of the labyrinth has traditionally been understood as symbolic of the process of rebirth, or resurrection. We go in to go out; we descend to ascend; we go back to what many think of as the womb, pictured by ancients as labyrinthian and connected to the intestines, the gut of the being.

Why Walk the Labyrinth Today?

One of the key reasons people walk labyrinths today is to have the experience of the simultaneity of past and present. In walking the labyrinth we link with other cultures and eras. We also link body and soul; we simultaneously have a physical and spiritual experience. We make metaphors work for us. The journey is one foot after another, and it is a path to the holy place inside us.

There are no wrong turns in a labyrinth; pilgrims always get home. Likewise, there are no wrong uses of the labyrinth; people in all times in all ways have made their own use of its geometry. History itself is a permission to use the labyrinth in one's own way. The labyrinth has only one path, so there are no tricks to it and no dead ends. It confirms our faith that hope exists in the universe. Its order is multifaceted, multiphrased, and multiexperienced, even as the labyrinth implies a singular path. Because so much of our daily experience is quite chaotic, and was so for ancient peoples as well, the labyrinth is a hopeful sign of order emerging from apparent chaos.

Labyrinths tell us who we are, internally and externally. Labyrinths are threads and cords that have not only biological but ontological significance. Thus, many of the labyrinth myths tell the story of the connectedness of people who imagine they are in danger, like Ariadne, who uses a thread to help Theseus find his way from death back to life. Modern uses rarely involve such explicit danger, even though the spiritual life often emerges in response to a sense of danger. We know something is not right. We know we have a kind of hero's journey we must undertake, one to find our true self or an authentic sense of God. We know we need courage, and we know we need guidance.

In labyrinths, whether ancient or modern, we walk in and we walk out. We coil and we uncoil. We do so both physically and spiritually. The body and the spirit experience an intentional, simultaneous outing. We walk a path. It is both a spiritual path and a physical path—not either/or, but both/and. Our spiritual journey and our physical journey are united. When walking the labyrinth, we get comfort because we find ourselves on the Way. We do not have to act as if it is the same way for all people. Instead, we should think of it as our way.

No brief history can do justice to the form's persistence in time, down through the current moment, when there is good reason to believe that the form of the labyrinth is being more rapidly reproduced than ever before in history. However, the form can do justice to the history, and it does—by showing a certain timelessness in time.

Part One

Approaching the Labyrinth

DONNA SCHAPER

A brick labyrinth.

ONE

The Labyrinth Revival

WHY LABYRINTHS? WHY ALL OF A SUDDEN ARE PEOPLE everywhere walking the labyrinth? Those who walk give these answers: Because people are lost. Because the chaos is too much without the order of form. Because we enjoy the multifaith possibilities of the experience. Because it is an ancient ritual form available for modern use. The labyrinth is an archetype, reminding us that many people have felt lost and have searched for the Way.

The revival of interest in walking the labyrinth as a spiritual practice joins the current revival of interest in spirituality in general. As the popular press tells us, the fastest-growing area of interest in the country today is in that nebulous field called *spirituality*. If religion is defined simply as ultimate concern, then spirituality is an action or practice of paying attention to matters of ultimate concern. Labyrinths lead us to a center, where we hope we can find the Sacred.

Defined as it often is in contrast to religion, spirituality is more inner, more cyclical, more personal, less institutional, more informal, more horizontal than its parent, religion.

Religion is more likely to be outer in expression, formal in nature, institutional and collective in form, and more "vertical," often believing that it is "right"; spirituality is much more conditional. It is not as interested in right and wrong ways to worship as it is in the worshiping itself. Spirituality can thus be considered a "horizontal" practice, something we do ourselves, aware that it is simply human and only pointing to the Divine.

People today use the labyrinth in ways that are more spiritual than religious. People are interested in spirituality and labyrinths because they have often become disconnected from and disenchanted with traditional forms of religion. Maybe it is a millennial fatigue; maybe it is just what happens when worlds collide and turn and change. We link way back in order to go forward, as in the motion of labyrinth walking. We go back to ancient spiritual symbols to ease our fatigue at how long we have already walked, how far we have yet to go.

When Julia Ward Howe wrote in the last century that she was "tired, tired, tired, way down into the next century," she was talking about the struggle to abolish slavery. Now, many of us can identify with her statement without so obviously grand a mission. When we complain of fatigue, we are more often talking about the two-career family, demanding children, lengthy commutes, or lack of down time.

Staying awake is hard! Spiritual practice helps us to stay alert. Many people, regardless of age, class, race, or gender, are physically exhausted and spiritually empty. The ancient Christian monks called it *acedia*: bored to death while being bombarded with stimulation. Bored but bombarded. The Holy is still there in the busyness. Look for it; it has not gone. The only thing missing is our ability to see it. Labyrinths, fortunately, are a method of renewal that we can use easily.

In the book *Living the Labyrinth* by Jill Hartwell Geoffrion,[1] we learn how many different kinds of people are finding themselves drawn to the centering practice of labyrinth walking. Mainstream religious people, often considered "straight," are becoming interested in circles. Geoffrion speaks of walking the labyrinth as a journey to creativity. She shows how the sum of the experience is more than its parts, and how one can either be alone or be social in walking a labyrinth.

Other books tell us that more and more people are interested in finding access to the sacred from the vantage point of everyday life. The labyrinth is perfect for such spiritual adventures: it is flat, here, available, and findable. In *Spiritual Literacy: Reading the Sacred in Everyday Life* by Frederic and Mary Ann Brussat,[2] we find a context for the labyrinth. The Brussats summarize spiritual themes like relationships, creativity, and nature. In the section on leisure, we hear a Sufi teacher tell us that "all the qualities of a spiritual teacher can be found in a person who can cook an egg perfectly." In the section on things, we read Ernesto Cardenal saying that things are simply examples of "God's love." Nancy Burke, in the section on service, talks about healing: "It is hard to know which collapsed first, my soul or my vein." Then she tells the story of a ten-year-old fellow cancer patient who showed Burke a hole in her abdomen. The child said, "You should have gotten one of these" and proceeded to give Burke a healing touch, saying, "You can take it."

What these illustrations from a spiritual encyclopedia show us is that people need spiritual aids, things, or pictures to help them find God. The labyrinth is an exquisite thing, which is used imaginatively as a thing or an object to help us find God.

Labyrinth walking also meets the need of our current age for user-friendly spirituality. We may not be able to get to church, temple, mosque, or zendo regularly, but we can walk a labyrinth any time we can find one.

Labyrinth walking is also a friend to the person who prefers the casual rather than the formal. It is both a necessity and a luxury. A spiritual practice that does not require anything, labyrinth walking is elegantly simple. We might even say chic simple—and there is no doubt its very trendiness is part of its appeal. Rather than being embarrassed at how much humanity loves a fad, we might enjoy being part of one.

Labyrinth walking also accompanies the way that culture has become more flowing and less static. The Dutch architect Rem Koolhas says that we live in a time of flow, not just space and movement, not just "getting there." We increasingly need to develop a psychology and spirituality of flow. Labyrinths are flows that emerged originally in the world of time and space.

Many American spiritual communities are now making their own portable labyrinths. Kathy Musser, a founding director of the Labyrinth of Guild of New England, says that making the thirty-foot canvas labyrinth for her church was in itself a remarkable experience in community building. And now having the labyrinth available for walking on a weekly basis has been a wonderful opportunity for midweek prayer and meditation, not only for the church members but also for people in the larger community. Groups from other churches have come, youth groups come, parents bring their children and children bring their parents. Musser has been amazed at the response. It released a lot of creative energy. People walk the labyrinth and return with poetry, pottery, or music. The labyrinth is a real inspiration.

Community of Hope United Church of Christ, in Madison, Wisconsin, has both a portable folding labyrinth as well as a permanent one on the ground outside. The First Congregational Church in Appleton, Wisconsin, finds that its labyrinth attracts people who might not otherwise be drawn to worship. "It speaks to unknown parts of ourselves," says Jane Weeden, associate pastor there. She calls the labyrinth a "walking faith" or "a pattern with a purpose."

The Sunflower Labyrinth at Annie's Garden Center in Sunderland, Massachusetts, is not affiliated officially with any spiritual tradition but is open to the public for anyone who wants to walk it, anytime. A drive past it around the time of the solstices or equinoxes will find it filled with people walking it—from self-identified Neopagans to Christians and Jews who simply feel moved to celebrate the earth's cycles.

The First Congregational Church of Akron, Ohio, began its labyrinth project with months of education and exploration on the meaning of labyrinths. First Community Church of Columbus, Ohio, has an outdoor labyrinth made "to enable the meditative practice of walking a sacred path to be accessible to anyone at anytime." A sweet pea labyrinth resides in Maricopa County, Arizona. At the ecumenical Kirkridge Retreat Center next door to Columcille, there is a labyrinth made with native stone markings. In California, the most well-known and popular American labyrinth of all is found in Grace Episcopal Cathedral on San Francisco's Nob Hill.

At the second World Parliament of Religions, held in Cape Town, South Africa, a labyrinth was set up and walked by people of every imaginable faith. Sikhs joined Hindus, who walked alongside Jains and Catholics, Episcopalians and Jews, Muslims of every hue and variety, and Buddhist monks sporting cell phones. You can walk while talking or you can walk in silence. There is no one, universal right way to walk the labyrinth, but you might want to find the right way for you and do it, according to your own faith.

There are thousands of labyrinths open to the public across the United States. (See Appendix B for a sampling.) There are also many private labyrinths that are open to you with just a phone call. You may also choose to create your own. We have one mowed into the large meadow in our backyard. A friend faxed us the plans of the labyrinth at Chartres. My husband and son started measuring as soon as it came through; for them it was a mathematical event as much as a spiritual one. Using a string on a piece of wood like a compass, made large by the processes of multiplication, they then mowed the shape of the labyrinth in the yard and placed a rock smack dab in the middle of it. Our measurements and those of Chartres' labyrinth are exactly the same, but they would not have to be. We got lucky—tilted just slightly east to west, the Chartres size fits into our meadow. (See Appendix A for simple directions for creating your own labyrinth.)

The children walk it. The neighbors walk it. The dogs walk it. We hold birthday parties and weddings there. On the last full moon of the last century, we let a child lead us through it while music played from the porch. What were we doing? Ritualizing the end of the century in a form as old as many centuries.

Now, we are not the "type" for a labyrinth in the back-yard. We are more the quick-chicken-recipe, van-driving-late-to-the-soccer-practice type. But there it is, in our backyard, reminding us that we are both lost and found, fragmented and whole, puzzled and sure. I use it more than the rest of the family does, although I have found others out there surrepti-tiously. It takes about twenty minutes to walk the whole way in, then twenty minutes to walk out. Because of the slight tilt of the hill on which it sits, it constitutes good exercise. Some-times I pray while walking; sometimes I sing. Sometimes I go right to the center and sit. (Some of my friends are sure that I take my laptop and cell phone out there from time to time, but I am keeping those uses a secret.)

I do not know if I am doing the labyrinth walk right. I just know that when I do it, I feel more whole, less fragmented, more sure, less worried.

One year I had my birthday party in the middle of the labyrinth. Fourteen friends walked it with me, and then we sat in a circle and talked. The only requirement for this party was that everyone wear a hat, and everyone did. My daughter was scared to death that a bunch of middle-age women were going to walk the labyrinth nude, wearing only hats. I kept the fiction going on as long as possible. The most fun I have in the labyrinth is at night, when there is a full moon. Last summer I enjoyed watching the fireflies from its center. I still remember that birthday with hats. And only last week, one of the women told me she needed another walk. Her son had just committed suicide.

The labyrinth is an ancient tool for contemplation and inner cultivation. It is also an ancient symbol of the archetypal feminine, the spiraling circle, the nonlinear way. The many turns to the left and the right reinforce an integration of the left and right hemispheres of the brain. It is a symbol of spiritual quest and of the journey to the heart. In a labyrinth, you cannot get lost; you always get home. No matter how "outside" you feel, you can still get in. No matter how peripheral, you can still get to the center.

In fact, most labyrinths turn you to the farthest ring just before they bring you in. Some experts believe that there is only one way to create a labyrinth. As far as I am concerned, you do not have to do anything in a labyrinth. A labyrinth is a device to help people find God, no more and no less.

Labyrinthian is not considered by everyone to be a positive term. For many the very twisting and turning is a nonharmonic spiritual experience. Novelists commonly describe the city in labyrinthian terms.

> To the ancients, the labyrinth connoted paths of intricate deviation leading eventually to the center for the initiated from which demons were excluded by the very device of

the labyrinth. In the Middle Ages that center still held in the guise of walled towns with a centrally-located church giving order to the whole complex. In the nineteenth century that center begins to be eclipsed by secular institutions and by the twentieth century, novels question even the validity of presupposing that a center can be found.[3]

In the twenty-first century, we want more center, less periphery, more unity, less fragmentation. Labyrinths are spiritual devices that help people to achieve these spiritual objectives.

Labyrinths are spiritual homing devices. They are just tools and must be treated that way—as opposed to idolatrously or as things that are holy in themselves. They take us to the Holy; they are not the Holy. Labyrinths are a form of spiritual travel. Many people keep trying to find their way back home, to a simpler, more childlike place. All the way home, we hum the tune, "You Can't Go Home Again," but we keep putting one foot in front of the other anyway. It is a good thing about us humans that while seriously complicating our existence, we are also hell-bent on simplifying it. It is one of the contrary strains and one of those things that make us who we are.

One danger in spiritual travel is the failure to find what you are looking for. Another is disappointment at what you see. A third is the discovery that life elsewhere is pretty much the same as it is back home. Travel proves as nothing else can that a central ambiguity people face is the longing to be at home while away, and the longing while away to be at home. This doubleness is a surprise only to the fainthearted; to those who understand the powers of the Spirit and that of storied places, it is simply confirmation. There are enormous similarities between home and away, in and out, even if we do not have to make our own bed or do our own dishes. Regular travel often demonstrates that all we need is right at home even though we had to go away to find that out. The labyrinth often makes similar input: we go back to where we started, but as a different person.

"In the middle of my journey, in the middle of the woods, I lost my way." So wrote Dante in the *Divine Comedy*. Life is about getting lost and getting found, about getting far away from home and finding our way back. Labyrinths help to model these journeys: we get home by going there, and we discover at the end of the circled journey that we have been there all along.

Another gift of the labyrinth is its capacity to provide a way and a place to live an interior life in a strange place. It is not home, but it leads to home. We can be at home anywhere, even as we flow in and out of time zones.

Labyrinths are also for people who have graduated from therapy. If you are one of many of us who are taking up things with God and not just the psychologist, labyrinths can help. They bring us to subjects like exile and return, center and fragment, out and in. They bring us to psalmlike words—evoking the world and the power of the ordinary spiritual struggle. First, metaphorically, we feel lost; then we are found. There is an amazing grace at the heart and home of a labyrinth.

Labyrinths are also useful for people who are tired of words. The finest speech does not come from the tongue. If you want to go deep, and go deep slowly, and if words have let you down, labyrinths can help. Labyrinths are also for another kind of people: those of us who know that we need healing but cannot seem to move out of the world of confusion. Labyrinths by their very circularity focus us. As the title to Richard Carlson's book says, "Don't sweat the small stuff ... and it's all small stuff." Spiritual people pay attention to the details but do not get overwhelmed by them. Focus is one of the great gifts of great people. They seem to be able to concentrate, to pay attention, to hear their own depth and to follow it. The power to heal is the power of focus. It is to live from the place that really matters.

Many of us are paralyzed in and by confusion. Gadding about is one of the temptations we all face. We flit. We have what Buddhist meditators call "monkey mind." We wander from one room to another, looking for our lost glasses, the telephone, or the gym bag. The confusion is unnecessary. Labyrinths order the monkey in our mind. They calm us down. They clarify and focus us.

Finally, labyrinths link body and soul. They are an embodied spirituality. More and more people insist on linking mind and body, body and spirit, spirit and mind. In *The Anatomy of the Spirit: The Seven Stages of Power and Healing*,[4] Carolyn Myss addresses those of us who find ourselves well enough but would like to be even more well. She demonstrates the parallel teachings of the major religions and shows how they each advise seven core truths. Following both parts of the body and parts of the spirit, she shows how they interconnect. She shows how our bodies and our souls are linked, are of a piece, and how by paying attention to all the events in our lives and listening carefully to our bodies we are on the path to a holy wellness.

Walking the labyrinth lets us practice a spirituality that brings our bodies with us. We intuitively know that we need a circle, a pattern of out and in, an exile and a return. Our bodies know better than our minds that we want this kind of patterning for our somato-psyches. Labyrinths are for people who want embodied spiritual practices. Whether we want to rid ourselves of fatigue or confusion, or simply to live in our body and from there to pay attention, labyrinths help.

Why are labyrinths being laid out in parking lots of churches, recreation rooms in senior centers, and lobbies of hospitals? Why are popular magazines like *Time, Woman's Day, Town and Country*, and the Smithsonian's *Muse* featuring stories about them? Maybe it is because they are safe—places where people cannot get lost. Maybe it is because walking the labyrinth helps us to get home. Maybe it is because walking the labyrinth helps us to find the center—the center of ourselves, the center of our lives, the center of our world. Maybe it is because by finding *a* center, *the* center, *our* center, we become centered.

A labyrinth mowed into the author's backyard lawn.

TWO

The Absolute
Meets the Ancient

WHAT LABYRINTHS DO

WHAT LABYRINTHS DO BEST IS TO LINK THE OLD TO the new. We can walk them today and feel quite modern while hearing the echoes of many feet behind us. We are not the first to want a way home, nor will we be the last.

Today the global and the local shake hands: we discover in a dozen time zones that people have used words and symbols to remark on their experience. Sometimes life appears like a gigantic flea market of faith, a yard sale of Grandma's clothes spread all over the lawn, people picking through and taking just what they like. At other times we are surprised at the great themes of the faithful: love for those who suffer, the power of God, the absoluteness of the Divine, the certainty of order in creation, the sure destination of the Divine toward home, whoever he, she, it, or they is—the certainty that all seven billion plus of us matter. From these themes come what we know of justice and peace and the genuinely good life.

The big mix need not be a giant beige religion that covers everyone, but a brilliant and dynamic collision of passionately held convictions. An ecumenism of the heart will precede anything like a new faith. Labyrinths are a good tool for this postdenominational moment, when we are not where we were, but we are not yet where we are going, either. Labyrinths are genuinely ecumenical while simultaneously demonstrating the great themes of many faiths. If anything, past and future, global and local are linking at an accelerated pace. While some postmodernists would like to find in the acceleration of knowledge something that offends the great mysteries of faith, wanting to believe that chaos is just chaos, others are not afraid of the cynicism. Instead, some of us find these assaults on the ways we understand faith a challenge that we can walk through, walk around, and walk out of.

Walking the labyrinth helps seekers to find a pattern in the chaos and to see the pattern of the chaos. We do not claim something that is more than *just* a text or *just* a story or *just* one account of faith; instead, we like the mix of stories that constitute humanity. We like the twists and turns that history and peoples have taken. We walk our talk, and we talk our walk. We know there is an Absolute, anciently conceived in different ways, but we do not need to claim that it is *our* absolute. Nor do we think of it as *just* an absolute. Instead, we simply honor the patterning of chaos that Someone has done. We walk the circle.

Bodies can synthesize what heads can only distinguish. Walking is often mightily preferable to talking. Some say the perfect religion will be mostly music. A Catholic friend tells me that priests today are torn between the dual responsibility to preserve tradition and to have it evolve. They and we want to know if it is possible to embrace diversity without also embracing relativism. In the labyrinth, yes; in the sanctuary and denomination, the cathedral and the mosque, the challenge may be greater.

Not only have religious words and texts taken a beating in the postmodern period, so has religious space itself. Rem Koolhaas claims that technology has replaced public space with virtual space—that the only urban space that matters in our time is the one we connect to on the computer. If that were true, Times Square would be a quaint and empty relic. While actual space is not gone, it *is* threatened by virtual reality.

Labyrinths bridge this chasm between the ancient and the modern. They are popular precisely because they are part of the transformation of sacred space and ancient texts that is happening today. They bridge public and holy space, inner and outer space. They bridge the *sacer*, the site of the unexplainable, with *profanus*, the site of the explainable.

Today, sacred space is both more expansive and more dilute. Labyrinths accommodate this transition. You can put one down anywhere—or you can travel all the way to France and walk the one at Chartres. Either act allows you to fully participate in the meaning of the labyrinth.

People have widened their claim to worship in nature—hiking a mountain, for example, rather than sitting in a designated worship space. Worship is as portable as our food and phone, as comfortable as our sneakers, as accessible twenty-four hours a day as the Internet. Many Protestant churches now are "dressed down," creating an even more homogeneous world. Without "costumes" to distinguish one kind of event from another, modern believers enjoy the comfort of the continuous. Believers blend both time and space: they have a toe in the water of faith and are moved to worship by normal human factors, ranging all the way from the stress in their own lives to secular tragedy and public spectacle. People worship more now, not less—but they worship outside the sacred time and space categories of more traditional faiths.

Not only has the place of worship changed, but the time of worship has also changed. The industrial term *movable parts* may best describe the worship habits of those today who are no more or less desperate for the sacred than their forebears were. Sunday has changed, and those of us in the Christian institutional religious community are just beginning to figure out how to respond to the changes. Blended marriages, the demise of blue laws, sporting events, the two-career family, and the Internet have each had their way with Sunday as some of us used to know it. Those of us accustomed to cultural support for the time and space of our piety are quite threatened by its absence.

Labyrinths help seekers and believers to make the transition into new kinds of space and new kinds of texts. Blended populations and portable time and space do not result in an absence of spiritual practice. Instead, they result in an expanded, if secularized, practice of the sacred.

Many of the most moving (and easily caricatured) examples of liturgical space today happen around tragedy. People build altars with rocks and flowers on the site of the Oklahoma City bombing; the Methodist church there has struggled to keep up with the ritualized behavior of people who stayed outside of the church to find a spiritual ritual. Coming *into* the sanctuary was something some could not do; they stuck to the street, the edge, the outer sanctuary steps. There was more sacred space—an inner and outer sanctuary—but it was more dilute. The inner space was diluted by the outer world's lack of entrance, and the steps were not enriched by the liturgical practice of the more disciplined inner space. The quick placement of flowers is no rival to the lengthy recital of communal prayers—and both inner-ring and outer-ring communities are intensely aware of the absence of the other in their space.

Crosses erected on the hill over Columbine High School were ritually taken down and put back up—not in an argument about the separation of church and state, but in an argument about whether there is any hope. The conversation among the students went beyond the typical quarrels of traditional religious groups over the placement of religious symbols in public places, the conversation was about a spiritual matter. The cross offended them because it implied hope, and they found that level of hope, so soon after the devastation, to be phony. Thus, the putting up and the taking down of the crosses represented the web and weave of social and spiritual conflict about religion, practiced in public. Labyrinths dissolve the distinctions between inner and outer, making way for new textual meanings.

Those of us who enjoy traditional denominated faith, like myself, understand the threat of the outsiders to organized religion. We are legitimately concerned about the future of the institutions we love. When so much is potentially so sacred, even if contested, there is a real threat to the genuine. Why build cathedrals at all if a street corner will do? The new faith has no parents: in fact, it rejects its parents. It is illegitimate, impure, mixed, miscegenated. It uses expanded and diluted spaces and fragmented times to win its independence. Labyrinths, and other postdenominational spiritual practices, unintentionally threaten organized religion. Only the naive think they do not.

Still and nonetheless, despite the threat to the children of organized faiths, the labyrinth connects these fragmentations, making the way for new and different kinds of unities based in the ancient ways. Organized religions used labyrinths in their own pasts; in all likelihood they will accommodate them again.

As easy as it is to be dismayed by flower altars on city street corners, as easy as it is to bemoan the loss of historical liturgical expressions, as easy as it is to be frustrated by Columbine cross maneuvering, there is a silver lining in these clouds, even a glimmer of a new revelation. If people make liturgy themselves in their own way, can much be lost in returning the act of praise and petition to the work of the people? The transfer of power has just begun: the forms are not mature, but liturgical power no longer belongs only to the properly credentialed. The spiritually subjugated are winning. The people are back in charge.

I do not want to minimize the losses, which include the beauty of the music of the ages made for sanctuaries, from chants to Bauhaus. Chartres could simply not be made today—if for no other reason than the lack of focused attention and near impossibility of cooperation. When I think of monks copying the ancient holy words of the scriptures, and then I learn that many fourteen-year-olds today think that the Book of Jonah is in the New Testament, I cringe. My heart breaks, but stuffing the genie—or God—back in the bottle is simply not possible. People cannot be forced to love beauty, especially credentialed beauty. Instead, we have a divine invitation to create open space for the new expansion of God's revelation.

Labyrinths are not so much relativistic or syncretistic as they are bridges to new forms and new ways. We walk them rather than talk them. Many of us multifaith, postdenominational people are uncomfortable with established religions. *Saturday Night Live* is not just kidding about the "church lady." The skit would not have been so funny if it wasn't solidly based in reality.

We realize today that God may like humble walks in ancient circles better than moral superiority. James Galway, the Irish poet, said that his religion was a noose around his neck and that it kept him from hanging. He identifies the tension of spiritual living today: we want to be safe, and we want to be free. Both are possible—but only in expanded spiritual frameworks, broken open by no other action than that of the Holy itself (herself, himself, itself, the Quark, the Force; the God whom some call Jesus, some call YHVH, some call Allah, some call Breath, some refuse to name; the God before whom there are no other gods). When we walk a labyrinth, we walk with thousands of human forebears who took their own trouble to the path and worked it out.

While wanting to be both free and safe, correct and open to correction, many of us genuinely enjoy both inner and outer pluralism. I delight in a world where it is not hard at all to meet a Zen-leaning Lutheran, a former Buddhist who is now Catholic, a Jew turned Quaker, or a Quaker turned Jew. The labyrinth helps me to do something with everybody that I do not have to do *right*. It helps me to hear the ancient texts in a new way.

Blaise Pascal long ago offered a way to speak of this full, lateral, relational pluralism when he said, "Nature is an infinite sphere whose center is everywhere, whose circumference is nowhere." No longer can we hear the ancient texts of our own faith as absolutely absolute; instead, we can hear them with others' texts. It helps us to relearn how to be faithful people. It helps to remind us that the center is everywhere. Not one of us is normal and the rest abnormal; not one of our faiths is best and the rest inferior or relative to it. There is no "other" faith; there are many faiths. The center is everywhere.

In today's spiritual environment, we are having simultaneous inner and outer battles over pluralism, blend and diversity, relativism and the Absolute. The labyrinth is a spiritual homing device that gives us the experience of solutions to these problems, if not the solutions themselves.

Raised as a Christian, I can hear my ancient texts in one of two ways. I can hear them as the absolute certainty and the only word of God, or I can take them for a walk in a roundabout way. They can be certainty for me, or they can be something I cannot control but with which I may and must move. My ability to move with my own historical faith as I walk with yours is deeply meaningful to me. Even when I walk my labyrinths alone, I know there is space for others. Labyrinth walking is a piety—a spirituality—not a theology or a faith.

Clearly, there is a new kind of piety now that people are making up as they go along. Private prayer joins public prayer as a place for the experimentation. People not only take to the streets with their own creative liturgical responses to tragedy, they also develop highly individualized, noninstitutional ways to worship. We are more pious than we realize. The labyrinth lets people walk together and separately without agreeing on everything. The very ancient nature of the labyrinth combined with the archetypal metaphor of its design draws us to absolutes that transcend any human constructs that have separated humanity into arbitrary religious categories for centuries. That is why labyrinths are so welcome today: they allow each of us to find our own center in our own way.

Walking the Sunflower Labyrinth at Annie's Garden Center, Sunderland, Massachusetts.

THREE

What Is Spiritual about the Labyrinth?

WALKING A LABYRINTH IS JUST WALKING IN CIRCLES, and it is a deeply spiritual practice. Labyrinths are both/and. They are neither just physical nor just spiritual. However, some labyrinth walks are less spiritual than others, and some are less physical than others. The blend is up to us. Sometimes we walk to walk. We move to move. We like the possibility that a spirituality may accompany a physicality. As great a saint as Augustine, one of the early leaders of the Christian church, believed that "all problems can be solved by a walk." As little a saint as I used to make major decisions by walking a hundred blocks in New York City. Why one hundred, and not two hundred—or ninety-nine? I made up the number, possibly the way others made up 666; I used a kind of magic on the walk—or, in more ancient terms, I ritualized it. By ritual, I mean something quite metaphorical and metaphysical: I made a decision as to the beginning and the end. I began with a problem; I ended with a problem solved. I made up my mind about certain limits and stuck to them. A labyrinth also gives us those limitations in a very expansive but chosen way.

Walking the labyrinth is a metaphysical, not a physical, practice—but it cannot be *meta-* until it is *physical*. One of the strongest appeals of the labyrinth is that it is a spirituality connected to a body. We do not have to leave our bodies behind to walk the labyrinth. They come with us.

One of the big words in modern theology is *embodiment*. People want to know if we can walk the walk as well as talk the talk: labyrinths answer that question yes, if in ever so modest a way. Labyrinths encourage embodiment rather than discourage it; that is a strong reason for their popularity among the new seekers.

Labyrinths are a physical-plus activity or a spiritual-plus activity. Before we can understand what is spiritual about them, we have to understand that they are also *just* physical. Labyrinths are, however, more spiritual than religious. They offer a distinction between religion and spirituality. They embody spirituality, not religion, and many people are "allergic" to religion today.

I asked my three teenagers if there was a difference between spirituality and religion. You will want to know why. They were refusing to go to church but agreeing to go to a church-sponsored camp. The sixteen-year-old said it was simple: "In church, you have to sit there—in spirituality, you can move around." My fourteen-year-old came along for the ride: "In religion, it's all God, God, God, and how God is good and we're bad. In spirituality, there is room for us."

Ernest Troeltsch, a German theologian at the beginning of the nineteenth century, predicted all this and more. He advised that churches and sects and mystics would be the three shapes of religion in the twentieth century. Mystics, he argued, would win out in the end because we were going to see a more inner religion develop. By the word *mystic*, Troeltsch did not mean someone who had visions; instead, he meant someone whose inner religious life was far more important than his or her outer religious life. "I can worship in a forest on Sunday as well as I can worship in a church," says one modern-day mystic.

Troeltsch also warned, grimly, that the ascendancy of the inner and the mystic would "make ethics impossible." Spirituality is a magnificent refuge for those who find ethics intimidating—and most people do in a rapidly globalizing economy, which thrives on the fact that both religions and sects have "terminal laryngitis." Who isn't ethically immature in a world where a rational, democratic nation dropped a bomb that wiped out thousands of people instantly? At some level, my teenagers join me in knowing that even the best nation ever is also the most potentially destructive. What that means about ethics and human development is not easy to assimilate, either spiritually or religiously, either inwardly or outwardly. Ethical intimidation is simply reading reality well. Not to be ethically intimidated would be foolish.

When we walk a labyrinth, or indulge any spirituality, we need to think about doing so from the inside out. That is, we need to be ready to go back to the big world where big issues are discussed. We do not use the labyrinth (or any spiritual practice) as a refuge as much as we use it as preparation.

Spirituality links the enormous powers of the secular world with the great quarry of religious tradition. Religious and spiritual practices can also make us capable of the ethical action we now find so intimidating. When we walk in a ritual way, in a labyrinth, we are preparing for our walk and way in the real world. We are just practicing.

The revival of devotional practice in daily prayers, prayers before meals, prayer shawls, devotional and spiritual reading—a revival of piety and interest in spirituality—represents our striving to find answers to some very basic questions.

Many of us want to become new and do not know how. Piety gives us a way to reframe our lives around God, with God at the center of the wheel. We experience ourselves as too tired to go on and too afraid to stop. Many of us are ready for piety, for forty days in the wilderness. We are ready to put our life picture in a new frame. We are ready to dive deep and come up with a fish in our mouth.

Piety is a new frame for ordinary life. A new frame is a new picture; it reorients the material. A new frame is a kind of resurrection, or resuscitation, or renewal. It is as good as a new outfit, as fresh as a haircut that works, as lively as a well-set table awaiting a well-cooked meal.

The writer Tillie Olson speaks of her life needing "margin." It had run into the walls of her frame. Artists and photographers insist that the empty space around an object defines it as much as the colored-in part. Piety is the rearrangement of the space in which we live. It is a look at context, at the air, at the nothing that is ours. It is just practice.

We get in our own way, especially when we try to change our lives and become the people we were meant to be. The more we reframe, the more the spirits convulse within us. Sometimes the harder we try to be ethical human beings, the worse we become. The very anxiety of our effort gets in our way.

In a discipline of devotion, prayer, or song, we can repattern ourselves. We can put new songs in our heads rather than the old negative "can't do" tapes. The best definition of prayer I have ever heard is that it is seeing the world from God's eyes and not from our own. When somebody says that poverty is necessary, you smile in prayer and say, "No, it's not." When somebody acts as though he or she were God, you relax in prayer and say, "No, you're not." When somebody suggests that you deserve to suffer because you have been bad, you say, "No, I don't."

If we are going to have to go deep in prayer regularly in our normal, everyday life, we had better develop a pattern of regular prayer to support our dives to the deep when we need them just to carry on. To live a life without prayer—to eat meals and say no grace before them, to go to sleep without saying goodnight to God's larger meanings, or to drive through autumn leaves and not be aware of God—is to live in poverty. It is spiritual poverty, spiritual hunger, and spiritual homelessness. It is to risk living centered only on yourself, and that is worse than living on welfare. Living centered on God, becoming more and more capable over time of seeing the world from God's perspective, is a form of wealth. It is a form of being rich. It is a form of piety.

Piety and spirituality are so good, so beneficial, so practical that it is hard to whisper even a slight complaint against them. However, those of us who live in the great flea market of faith need to "ping the crystal" on the goods in this market just to make sure they are not fakes. How would we know the real from the phony? We know if walking the labyrinth has helped us by how we behave when we return from its ritual pattern to our so-called real life. (By the way, the very spiral of the labyrinth calls into question these alleged differences between our real life and our ritual life. Our ritual or prayer life may be more real than we think; our daily lives may be less real than we think.) Ethical behavior, the work of justice, the consequence of peace, the inability to be anything but fully compassionate—these fruits of the spirit bubble outward from our deepened interiors. They spiral from inside to outside.

What is wonderful about the embodied spirituality of the labyrinth is that it uses our bodies. Bodies tell limited stories well because bodies are limited. They go less than a hundred years, with most parts falling apart quite before then. Bodies tell little stories, not big ones. They let in the little goblins, like fear or fainting. Labyrinths circle these small stories into something we can call a piety or a spirituality.

We just have to keep on walking. We will get somewhere.

Once we were hurt by a group at church or synagogue or mosque, so now we never get close to anybody at church or synagogue or mosque again; that way we will not get hurt again. Once we were laughed at by a coach, so now we never go out on a field again. Once we were divorced or abused or raped, so now we are so careful that we make ourselves a prisoner in our own apartment. Once we got so mad at our child that we almost beat him or her, the way our parents beat us. For many of us, something that happened long ago is still happening. We stopped our story, or a piece of our story, because it was really so bad that we decided we did not want to write through it or around it or under it or over it. Loss becomes our ruler.

You can actually see these blockages in some people's bodies: hesitation, circling, wandering, pent-upness, spine-lessness, brokenness, bent-overness; eyes that cannot focus on anyone, ears that cannot really hear anyone, mouths that cannot really say anything, hands that cannot really touch anything, feet that cannot walk anywhere; souls capable of enormous feeling—homeless souls—looking for a body to inhabit, a temple in which to grow towardbetter endings. These people need a circle in which to keep their story going; these people could use a walk in a labyrinth.

One of the great mistakes that mainstream religions today have made is in thinking that religion is only a spiritual matter. Such people do not want to hear about anything material or physical when they come to God. As long as you feel good about God, then what you do with your money or your body or your house or your car is extra. It is neither godly nor ungodly because religion is spiritual. Nothing could be further from the incarnate truth of most faiths. For example, there is the so-called incarnate truth of Jesus Christ. To incarnate is to embody, to put *carne*, or flesh, around God. That is what we Christians believe that Jesus did: he became flesh and dwelt among us, he incarnated God. Jews similarly think of Israel as the embodiment of God, as God's actual action in history—flesh-and-blood stuff, not ethereal history but genuine history.

Christians say about heaven that we experience not just a resurrection of the soul but also a resurrection of the body. Christians also believe that the Holy Spirit inhabits our bodies as though our bodies were temples, sacred enclosures for the Holy Spirit. A holy place for the Holy Spirit—that is, our flesh and our blood and our veins and our feet and our spines, a holy place.

If you can go far enough to understand that faith is a physical-spiritual phenomenon or a spiritual-physical one— that it is always both and never just air or light or breath, but also something you can touch and feel and bodily experience—if you can jump this hurdle, then you can really start having fun in labyrinthian places.

If you can accept the Jewish claim that God is active in history—dirty, limited history—then you are ready for the labyrinth. You are not afraid of the way the body accompanies spirituality or spirit. You are ready to somatize the psyche and the spirit as well as psychosomatize. You are a somato-psychic, a soul not ashamed to have a body in a body not ashamed to have a soul. One of the members of one of my churches was still singing "doo, dah, doo, dah," after she could no longer dance, stabilizing herself with her walker with both hands and lifting only pointer fingers, days before she died. Glorify God with whatever body you have left. Bodies do not always feel good, sometimes they feel bad. Both good and bad bodies walk labyrinths, not just the good-feeling ones. Our bodies do not have to look like movie stars' or models' to glorify God in a stumbling kind of semisuccess. We can limp the labyrinth as well as walk it.

Our bodies are the temple for the spirit. The physical and the spiritual are intertwined in most ancient faiths: you cannot speak of one without the other. Likewise, neither spirits nor bodies die: they resurrect and reincarnate. The glorifying is in the glorifying, not in the beauty or perfection of the person or body. Ritual takes on reality in many different ways.

Sometimes the Holy Spirit does not know what to do so much that we are advised to simply take a walk. It does not even have to be in a labyrinth, but if it is, we get the ancient promise of a sure way home to accompany us.

A canvas labyrinth rolled out on a gymnasium floor.

FOUR

Spiritual Authority
in the Labyrinth

THERE IS A BUMPER STICKER THAT ENCOURAGES ALL who read it to "Question Authority." It is unlikely that the author of that proclamation was referring to spiritual authority, but one never really knows about the theology of bumper stickers.

How do you decide what to believe or not believe about God?

Spiritual authority in religious circles is one of those great issues that keeps scholars and theologians debating, defining, redefining, and writing treatises. Except for scholars, theologians, and seminary professors, most people do not spend much time worrying about it.

Authority is the ultimate source or resource that lays claim to describing the nature and acts of God. For example, for Roman Catholics the ultimate authority on spiritual matters is the Church headed by the pope. For Jews, the ultimate authority rests in the Torah, the first five books of the Hebrew

Bible—Genesis, Exodus, Leviticus, Numbers, and Deuteron-omy—and the collection of ancient rabbinic writings called the Talmud. For Muslims, the ultimate spiritual authority is the collection of recitations of Muhammad called the Qur'an. These are all sample authorities from traditional religion.

During the Protestant Reformation of the sixteenth cen-tury, much of the pulling and tugging that occurred as new denomination after new denomination broke away from its parent denomination was fueled by differing views on the issue of authority. Part of the Reformation's struggle was a shift in authority from the Church and the pope to scriptures, primarily the four books of the New Testament commonly referred to as the Gospels: Matthew, Mark, Luke, and John.

During the Reformation, which was accompanied by a changing worldview brought about by the Renaissance and followed by the scientific and industrial revolutions, individu-als began to name and claim their own unique experiences of God as their ultimate authority. Many people moved away from spiritual authority entirely and replaced it with a scien-tific authority.

For those exploring the labyrinth as a spiritual discipline, the age-old question arises: By what authority? By what au-thority is walking a labyrinth a potentially godly thing to do? If we walk to a newness and an openness and a way to love, then the walking is godly. If nothing much happens, we got a little exercise, we passed our time pleasantly. We "lit our own picture well," as André Gide put it. However, genuine piety, genuine spirituality, and genuine authority for the godly comes in the fruits, in what happens next.

When people today speak of wanting a spirituality, they mean that they want to practice the presence of God in their lives. They want rituals, they want culture. They want iden-tity in a group of other religious observers, but they do not want to be like "church people" or the Puritans or the pious.

They want to practice the presence of a kind, rather than a judgmental, God, in their lives, a God who opens us and makes us more capable of compassion. Phony gods close us down or leave us the same as we were when we started the relationship. Phony gods teach us how to be more functionally depressed; they reinforce the status quo. Real gods change us. Real gods break us open for love.

Labyrinth walking is one way to be pious, to have a spiritual practice without having to carry the burden of centuries of traditional religious authority. Without demeaning the grand traditions of institutional piety—the centuries-old complex of liturgies and prayers, hymns and linens, the gestures and habits of all our various faiths—simple labyrinth walking opens up piety as a point of view on life, of a way to be in the world.

There are other wonderful and equally simple pieties: prayers at meals or simply singing. In the myth of Orpheus in the underworld, a youth who sings with a voice of real sweetness descends into the depths of the earth to find his lost love, Eurydice. Along the way, Orpheus encounters a series of monsters and challenges. He discovers that with his voice alone he can overcome any obstacle. He tames monsters just by singing. Some people do yoga, others do tai chi. Labyrinths are one of many wonderful devices for practicing the presence of God, but they are hardly the only one.

The gift of the labyrinth in my life is that it has restored my spiritual sense of humor. It has given me a kind of clarity about how "large" God is. It has also given me a sense of how much life truly is a journey, a movement, or a process: from every point in the labyrinth, God and life look different. Every single point. Even though all the points are different, I like to pray the same prayer, which I learned a long time ago, at each one: "Let yourself be silently drawn by what you really love." This prayer opens, clarifies, and amuses me. It amuses me because what I really love is often quite silly. It is often quite less than what I thought it should be. I love recycling. I love homegrown lettuce. I also love justice and martinis. I should love more noble things, but I don't. I love fairly silly things. I do not need to be rich, I just need a salad and a drink from time to time. These completely satisfy me. Labyrinths help us not to dull and dumb down but to waken and sharpen. They let us see how silly, perhaps simple, we really are.

"Life shrinks or expands according to one's courage," said Anaïs Nin. So many of us are often scared because we have not looked up or back or forward in a long time. When we do look up, we get the courage we thought we had lost. When walking the labyrinth with others, I prefer silence, although many prefer conversation. I like the practice in many labyrinths of greeting each other with *namaste*—the Hindu practice of bowing with hands together as a silent acknowledgment of the God within the person we are encountering. The bow is simple but direct. It allows for communion in the solitary walk, but not too much, and that is what I prefer. Others may prefer something quite different. We each have the spiritual authority to prefer what we prefer.

How will you know if solitude or communion is best for you in your labyrinth walk? By the fruits. By what happens to you after you walk. Are you more open to both genuine solitude and genuine community after the walk? Often we do not know exactly what we need. A good question to take on a solitary labyrinth walk or to ask a friend is this: Do I need more solitude or more community in my life right now? Because so much of my work is with the least, the last, and the lost, I personally need the solitary space with God more than I need companionship. Others are quite different. Knowing that we know how different we are is often the largest sign of love and compassion we can give.

Labyrinths are not a spirituality that results in a chirping optimism, nor do they deliver us from all anxieties. They let us rest along the way, and they make a plain way on which we can walk. As E. B. White put it so well, "Always be obscure with clarity." Labyrinths are an inner method for an outer grace. They help us to find the Holy. Labyrinths help us with our posture toward life; they do not cure us so much as help us to stand up straight.

Life bends most people into funny shapes. Labyrinths help us get bent into shape, not out of shape. Posture is an attitude of the body. Poise is its source. Inner bends outer into shape. When we see a human standing upright, we know calm prevails. Inner commands outer.

Cultivating the inner is the best way to find the beauty of the human soul. Labyrinths cultivate the inner, which is the site of our authority. For our spiritual rest and recreation, we may walk a labyrinth, run one, or dance one. We may even trace one on the dirty windows of the cars in a parking garage.

In the Christian Scriptures (Luke 13:10–13), there is a story about a bent-over woman who approaches Jesus for healing. This woman may help us see the consequences of not cultivating our own inner spiritual authority. The bent-over woman made a mistake: she waited too long to be well. Everybody makes mistakes; most are simpler and less costly. The bent-over woman forgot. She forgot God. The powerful were delighted that she forgot, because that kept them in power. She consented to stoop—to assume a position of disempowerment—and thus to hide her authority.

What is the attitude of a stoop? It is a curving in, a sense of the self, and the self only, as providing safety. It is a sin: what Martin Luther actually described as sin *incurvatus in se*, curved in on ourselves. We miss the mark of our true humanity. We become small in a small way instead of small in a significant way.

Think for a minute of your own stoop. You know what it is. I know mine: my long waiting to be well. We all have stoops; some just show more than others. Why do we wait so long to receive God's power to be small and free, silly and simple?

One reason is usually that we do not want to become small at all. We want to follow the advertised instructions that we become big—and if not big, then God. Instead of fighting the powerful, most of us want to become one of them.

We bend funny. The labyrinth is a bending, twisting, turning shape. We know something of its authority when we stand up straight while bending to its form. Imagine an alternate script for your life—to straighten up and fly right, to be carried on the wings of a mighty God, one who guarantees our safety in any and all danger.

What makes us stoop? Is it a harm done to love when genuine courage would be to forgive and to love as though you had never been hurt?

Once I watched two men in the sixties holding hands wearing matching blinking ties on Christmas Eve in the back row of a church in Tampa, Florida. They were in love, they were loving. In many places these two men could not have shown their love; here they could. They were not stooping, crouching, or hiding. They had genuine spiritual authority.

Sometimes our stoop comes from aimlessness and a lack of focus rather than a lack of love. "God, save us from aimlessness and sin," we say often in my church. *Aimlessness* is not getting the word out about your passion to enough people so they can join in your parade, not fully knowing yourself or your limitations. *Sin* is missing the mark, being asleep at the switch, not figuring out what is going on, not consenting to partnership with God. Instead, we might be wise. We might look trouble straight in the eye. We might have made a plan and aimed for it. These are the kinds of tasks one can use a labyrinth to accomplish.

Sometimes the stoop in our spiritual authority comes from a harm done to our voice. I think of one singer's complaint that people always got mad at her for taking too many breaks. They would torment her to sing long, hard songs twice. She came to hate the people for whom she worked. Instead of singing for them, she lost her voice. She started to stoop, and her life turned to hate instead of love. Walking a labyrinth is not what everybody would recommend for people who are being silenced, but I would. It is a way to get back home to one's voice as well as to love and focus.

Any piety will do to accomplish these goals. The specialness that labyrinths bring is the assurance of home at the end of our journey. They circle us back and forth, allowing the energy to uncoil us, to straighten our backs, to walk taller. Authentic pieties unstoop us, they bend us back into shape. Again, that does not mean that all our problems are solved or all our griefs are over. Instead, we become people who can be joyful anyway; who are aware of the presence of God, anyway; who have a "joy no circumstance can alter," in the marvelous words of Evelyn Underhill.

The presence of God is the difference between joy and happiness. We can be happy without God, but we may not be joyful without God. Happiness is a checkbook that has money, a car that works, a good date for Saturday night. Happiness is the absence of major hassles, terrorism, or crime; happiness is a kid's getting good report cards and a spouse getting a raise. Happiness is something we know as enhancement or protection of our own lives.

Joy comes in the connection with another or with God. Joy comes as presence with God or as simply the presence of God, a presence many have experienced while walking or praying in a labyrinth. Joy can happen without money or a working car. Joy happens when we get to the core of life, to the center of our souls, to the center of the labyrinth, and realize that love is at the core. Joy befriends us; love accompanies us. The labyrinth is a lot about the core and the center and what is most important.

Naming our own experience of God is part of claiming the authority of our experiences of transcendence. I call my God Jesus or Christ because I was raised that way. The Dalai Lama has another name for what I call God; so does my husband's rabbi. When we experience the presence of God, God has a name for us. The actual name is not as important as the process of naming God. Even "Breath" will do. However, when God is close to us, we use names.

As we walk the labyrinth, we begin to find names for our God that bring meaning to our lives. I know a woman who has four children. Three of them have AIDS, and so does she. Her only wish is to outlive her three dying children so that she can comfort them as they leave this earth. She calls these dying children "morning glories." The name seems to be catching on for children who have AIDS. Like the flower, their life is brief but beautiful. This woman knows almost no happiness, but God is never far away from her. She knows the joy of the presence of God. Her fourth son, she says, will have to be taken care of by the future. I asked her where she got her faith; she said that she had no idea, but that without it she would already be dead. With it, at least she can enjoy what she calls the morning's glory. She has enough of the presence of God to make up her own names for what matters to her.

If joy is not something you know intimately, perhaps taking a walk in a labyrinth will renew your connectedness to God. You might consider behaving like a wave of joy. You might spread the joy you do know. Joy does not come only to those who suffer; it also comes to those who get acquainted with who God really is.

Consider the wave—not an ocean wave, but the sporting event phenomenon. Who starts it? How do fourteen thousand people get going all together in such a rhythm? Somebody must start it, so why not you or me? When it starts, people become receptive to taking instructions. They cooperate. We experience what computer types call a "positive feedback loop." Everything is amplified. We do not have any special power, but we experience joy, anyway. Waves really show you the difference between power and effect. In many situations, we do not really have any power, but we can have a big effect if the situation is set up right.

Labyrinths are like waves; they are like positive feedback loops. They show us how a small amount of power can have a large effect. Somebody starts every wave—it does not just happen. Somebody starts every wave. Somebody starts every circle.

Next time you are at a dinner party, and everyone starts making themselves feel good by putting down the people who are not there, watch what happens if you stop that wave and offer a replacement. Watch the next fight you have with your spouse or kids or neighbor. The same principle applies. Harness the positive power in the situation, and you may diffuse the negative. You might even have a big effect. You might even find that the effect of your action is magnified. You might even start to have a good time!

You probably do not think that you have what it takes to start waves of joy, but you do.

Because I believe these things about joy and spiritual authority, I walk labyrinths. They remind me of what I know and allow me the chance to take it for a walk. They show me how the circle grows into just what I need to be a compassionate person. They break me slowly open, the way one circle leads to another in the labyrinth. They spiritually open me—and that becomes my authority.

Part Two

Walking
the Labyrinth

CAROLE ANN CAMP

A very simple labyrinth made of bricks.

FIVE

Hearing the Dark

ELEMENTS OF THE LABYRINTH WALK

The path though known
Flows darkly, circling slowly
As a velvet river at midnight.
Familiar turns thrill the burning heart
With carefulness and searing joy.
The relentless walking begins.
What miracle this time
Escapes the darkness
To enlighten the Soul?
The misty shapes form just
Beyond the edge of vision
As the known flies by
Leaving only the silent self.
My soul at last is home.
                        —*Carole Ann Camp*

Walking is one of the various practices in use today for seekers of the transcendent experience. By walking a labyrinth, one can travel long distances in a small space. The labyrinth walk overflows with metaphor and meaning. The labyrinth represents a journey, a pilgrimage, a conscious taking of time to seek God. Many of the major stories in the Jewish and Christian scriptures involve journeys: Moses and his people journeyed toward the Promised Land, Joseph and Mary went home to Bethlehem to be counted, Jesus journeyed to resurrection, and Paul was converted on the road to Damascus—all powerful stories of journeys, journeys to find the Promised Land, to find home, to find God, to experience the Holy Spirit. We humans quest for God and for self-knowledge. We too want to experience the Holy Moment, the Presence of the Holy. One thing that is for sure, we cannot discover anything unless we look, we cannot move forward while standing still.

All over the world, people are searching for ways to express their deep desire to be on a journey to Oneness with the Holy of Holies—to experience, if only for an instant, that transcendent moment. The labyrinth in Grace Cathedral in San Francisco was originally painted on a very large canvas that was rolled out into the middle of the sanctuary. So many people were walking that labyrinth that the members of the church had to create a permanent one in the churchyard. They finally made a labyrinth rug for the sanctuary to replace the canvas one. Imagine hundreds of people of every shade and color, every profession and trade, taking their lunch hour, escaping from the hustle and bustle of San Francisco life, to walk the labyrinth.

On the surface, it may seem foolish to spend thirty to forty minutes walking up and down a painted canvas labyrinth, but that is not the point. The point is that a choice has been made; a spiritual discipline has been chosen; the presence of Spirit is being sought. Making the choice and taking that first step into the labyrinth is to risk discovering the mystery at the very center of our being. The good thing about labyrinths is that you cannot make a mistake. There are no wrong turns. You cannot get lost. Symbolically, what could be better than knowing that by staying on the path, by following all the turns, you will eventually find the center—the Holy of Holies?

When walking a public labyrinth, you are not on the path alone. Some people are just beginning the journey, while others are well on their way to the center. Some have found the center and are going back out into the world. In most labyrinths, you can see people walking in opposite directions at the same time. It is even possible, due to the design of the labyrinth, that those who are on the same path as you toward the center end up approaching you almost head-on, because of where they are on their journey. Sometimes one walks in the same direction as another, on a different part of the path— you journey together for a while but then go off in separate directions. On the labyrinth path, everyone is connected on a journey toward the same destination, the center, yet at the same time each has individual, separate experiences.

Another thing to keep in mind about labyrinth walking is that the journey out from the center is exactly the same distance as the journey in, and you *have* to come out. The journey inward prepares you for the journey outward. The inward path prepares you for the experience of the center; the outward path prepares you for your life in the world. Walking the labyrinth is not about escaping into the center and leaving the world, it is about experiencing Spirit in the center so that you can live in the world in a more blessed way. The labyrinth reminds you with every walk you take that your spiritual journey flows back and forth, from the outside to the inside, from the inside to the outside—both/ and, not either/or.

The choice is yours. You can choose to live your life as a maze or as a labyrinth—a maze with its confusions, wrong turns, dead ends, and false hopes, or a labyrinth with its many turnings, but none of them wrong, a path with sure and certain knowledge of reaching and experiencing the center, home.

The spiritual practice of walking the labyrinth is to walk in the ways of the Holy. In the Hebrew Bible, there is a story in the book of 1 Kings where King David is lying on his deathbed talking to his son, Solomon. David tells Solomon to be strong and courageous, and to walk in the ways of God. "Walk" in the ways of God. It does not matter what metaphor you use for God. It could be Creator, Holy One, Creative Life Force, Love, Mother, Father, Light of Light, Great Ruler of the Universe, Source of Life, or Mother Goddess. It does not matter whether you locate the Holy externally or internally, or a combination of both. To walk in the ways of the Holy means that you walk the walk as if today were the first day of the rest of your life and tomorrow the last. To walk in the ways of the Holy requires that you be strong in your inner self; that you equip yourself with truth, justice, faith, and courage; and that you be constant in prayer, alert and willing to persevere. Walking in this way is not like going out for a stroll, it is like going on a journey. It is intentionally choosing to be on a spiritual path. The call is to be on the move; trusting in the journey, open to seeing things in new ways. When one takes that first step in the labyrinth, one opens to the possibility of encountering the Holy of Holies on the path.

Just as there are no wrong turnings in the labyrinth, there are no right or wrong rituals to bring meaning to your walk. To help focus your intention, try some of the rituals in chapters 7–9. Most of the labyrinth rituals described in these chapters consist of seven parts: the Preparation, the Invocation, the Inward Journey, the Center, the Outward Journey, the Thanksgiving, and the Journal Reflection. This suggested ritual format is not the only possibility. It is offered here to start you on your journey.

As you begin to design your own rituals, remember that the labyrinth walk has two paths that are one path—the inward and the outward journey. In many of the rituals that follow you will notice that the inward and outward paths serve as two distinct parts of the ritual. Just as the two paths are actually only one path, the focus of each path is distinct. Remember to be as attentive to the outward journey as to the inward one.

Throughout history, people of every age and culture have at some time in their lives participated in various forms of prayer. Prayer is not confined to one religion or denomination. It does not have to be directed to one particular deity, like YHVH, Allah, Diana, Gaia, or Jesus. Prayer is not begging a cosmic god to run errands. It is a deliberate choice to focus your time and attention on growing in spirit. Being in prayer is to reclaim the depths of your center. Walking the labyrinth is body prayer—a prayer one does with the whole body. Walking to the center of the labyrinth is going to the very center of the self. Combining walking with some other form of prayer will deepen the peace you will experience in the center.

It is very important to remember that prayer in any form opens up the possibility of an encounter with God. Yet it is even more than that, it is also developing a relationship with God, one that has no bounds. This relationship cannot be forced on you or on God—it develops slowly over time and deepens with every step you take. By walking daily in a prayerful way, your connectedness to the Eternal Spirit will slowly and surely grow and strengthen. You do not need a rush of words to be in a state of prayer. Being in a state of prayer is more like an attitude than a set of correct words. Prayer is the total relaxation and the total surrender of the inner self to the Holy One. Imagine being held in the hollow of God's hands and resting in and on the Divine Presence. Being in a state of prayer is the total and absolute ability of letting go—letting go of everything, including all thoughts and worldly worries. Letting go into the depths of your inner world creates the feeling that you are being supported by a warm, velvety-soft darkness.

In that darkness, listen. Prayer is about listening. Listening to the dark does not mean that you will actually hear a voice talking to you, although some people do hear a still small voice in their minds. Others see images. Some just have a feeling. The five senses with which you come to understand and know the outer world are mirrored in your inner world.

We are familiar with words like *inner sight* or *insight*. The inner world is not limited to only one sense, inner sight. All five senses are mirrored inwardly. In addition to inner sight, we are blessed with inner hearing, inner touch, inner smell, and even inner taste. When you go into your inner world or your center, allow yourself to experience all of your inner senses. The more you practice listening to and in the darkness of your center, the deeper you will go into your center of being.

There is a danger about practicing this kind of contemplative and centering type of prayer while walking the labyrinth. If you really put yourself in a posture of being open to God's love and grace, you will experience God. When you meet God face-to-face in the darkness of your center or at the center of your labyrinth, the encounter is awesome.

Seeking the will of God should be a constant and conscious pursuit. As one grasps new truths and seeks to apply these truths on a regular basis, one will discover more of the divine intent for one's life. Prayer is that surrender to God.

Historically and traditionally, people created many forms and types of prayer: grace before meals, prayers of confession and absolution, prayers of thanksgiving. Some prayers are well known, like "Now I lay me down to sleep," or the familiar prayer of Jesus known as the Lord's Prayer; from the Hindu tradition, "*Sri Rama Jai Ram, Jai Jai Ram Om*" (To God, both Personal and Impersonal, both Truth and Power, Victory, always Victory); the traditional Tibetan chant "*Om mani, padme hung hri, om mani, padme hung*"; from Ezekiel's vision of the angels dancing around the throne of God, "*Baruch Kevod Yahuvah Mim Komo.*" People pray in a variety of ways: some stand, some kneel, some sit, some sing, and some dance.

Walking the labyrinth is another way to pray. The following prayers for your labyrinth walk are suggestions that can be prayed aloud or silently at various points on the journey. The list is not meant to be exhaustive but only to act as a catalyst for the development of your own prayer forms.

The Preparation: Before You Start

Although it is possible to run in and quickly walk around the labyrinth, by doing so you run the risk of missing the power that the labyrinth has for you. Just as you would dress up to go to a fancy ball by putting on clothes appropriate to the occasion, you may want to dress up for your labyrinth walk. Not only will you want to prepare your body, you will also want to prepare your mind for the experience. Not to prepare is to deny oneself the full experience. In the labyrinth at Grace Cathedral, walkers are asked to remove their shoes. This act is one simple way to ritualize the process of preparation—the act of taking off and putting aside. Before you walk the labyrinth, prepare yourself. Take off and put aside, in a conscious and ritual way, those things that may prevent you from the full experience. Some acts of preparing are like prayers of letting go and putting aside. The act can be as simple as taking off your shoes, or putting your purse, laptop, or backpack aside. The act could be taking off as many layers of clothing that climate and society allow or by putting on and wearing some special ritual clothing.

Preparation also includes preparing the labyrinth. If you are fortunate enough to have your own labyrinth, there are suggestions in the following chapters for ways to prepare your labyrinth for a particular ritual. If you are walking a public labyrinth, you may need to limit your preparation to vizualization.

Choose your favorite scripture or spiritual source for prayers and mantras that you can use in your labyrinth experience. The Psalms are what I use. They fall into several categories: psalms of praise, psalms of lament, psalms extolling the mighty acts of God, and liturgical psalms. I select a psalm that fits my particular need or mood. For example, if I am in a hard time in my life I pick a psalm of lament, like Psalm 23. If I am feeling grateful, I choose a psalm of praise, like Psalm 100. Whatever you use, take a written copy with you to your labyrinth. During your preparation time, read your passage aloud several times. Close your eyes and allow a word or phrase to come into your mind. Use that word or phrase as your mantra for the inward journey.

Take some time with your preparation. Your time of putting aside, letting go, and getting ready is very important. The more you are able to let go of and to put aside, the more your labyrinth walk will be able to lift you to the joys of ecstasy. The time of preparation includes preparing your body and mind as well as your labyrinth. If you are planning to lie down during the meditation time and you are walking your own labyrinth alone, you may want to place a foam pad in the center so your body will be comfortable for the meditation. When you have finished the physical preparations and before you start your walk, you may want to say or sing a prayer of invocation.

The Invocation before the Walk

Prayers of invocation are generally said at the beginnings of gatherings like public meetings, presidential inaugurals, commencements, worship services, or religious rituals. An invocation invokes or calls on God, Goddess, angels, saints, or the Spirit to be present at the function. If you believe that your God or Goddess is present with you all the time anyway, it may seem silly to ask specifically for your God or Goddess to be present on your walk. Your deity and your guardian angels are indeed always present with you, but the act of praying an invocation makes the person saying the prayer more aware of that Presence. Praying an invocation says to others and to God that you are really serious about this, that you are consciously and intentionally choosing to be on the spiritual path. An invocation can be as simple as saying, "Come, Holy Spirit." You may prefer a familiar prayer from your religious tradition. Invocations can also be in the form of a hymn, a song, or a dance.

The Inward Journey:
Walking the Labyrinth In

Once you have prepared and are ready to begin the inward journey, remember that to enter the labyrinth is to open yourself to profound and life-changing possibilities. The path inward to the center is the path that leads to the very heart of God—a path that leads to the very center of the self and to the very center of the universe. To put oneself on the path is to make the choice that you are now ready for the insights and the wisdom that your deity, the center, the Holy of Holies, has in store for you. This is not a frightening experience, but it is one that is filled with awe. As your feet touch the path, become aware of the path. Even if the path is some paint on a piece of canvas, forget the mechanics of the actual labyrinth that you are walking on and focus on the path—the path that is leading you inward, inward to a kind of transcendence. Allow others who may be walking the path to be there and not be there at the same time. With each step and with each breath allow your *self* to go deeper and deeper into the center—the center of you, the center of the universe, the center of God. Do not worry about whether you are walking in the right way or doing the ritual in the right way. There is no "right way," there is only your way. Allow yourself to walk as slowly as you can. Focus on *your* path.

To help you focus and to deepen your labyrinth time, you may want to say a mantra appropriate to your needs at that moment. The mantra is a single word or phrase repeated aloud or in your mind over and over again. When the word or phrase is repeated in harmony and timing with your breathing, the mind and soul begin to quiet. As you start to walk, join the pace of your steps with the rhythm of your breathing and the cadence of the mantra word or phrase. For example, if the chosen phrase is "Lead me, Lord," inhale and take a step on "Lead me"; exhale and take a step on "Lord." Keep repeating this phrase with every step you take until you reach the center. Another phrase that works well for a mantra for the inward journey is "*Shema Yisroel, Adonai Elohenu, Adonai E-had*" (Hear O Israel, the Lord our God, the Lord is One).

Many popular song titles can be said as mantras. It is not necessary to know all of the lyrics or the tune of the song. Try "Cry Me a River," "Give to the Winds Thy Fears," "I Believe in Love," "Let the Sunshine In," or "Love Is All We Need." If a song title or lyric comes to you on your way to the labyrinth, let it be your mantra for the walk.

You may wish to choose one mantra for your inward journey and a different one for the outward journey. For example, repeat the mantra "Lead me, Lord" as you travel on the inward path and "Guide me, Lord" on the outward path. Depending on your need or desire, the mantra may be a word or phrase from sacred texts or a word or prayer from a wise person.

One may also use a name or description of God or a great master, like Holy One, El Shaddai, Emmanuel, Allah, Muhammad, Jesus, Diana, or Isis. The mantra is a prayer suited to walking the labyrinth because it is easy to remember and because it allows the mind, body, and soul to act in harmony. If you come to the labyrinth with a specific need, choose a mantra that is appropriate to that need. If your body is in need of healing, you may want to choose "Heal, me, God." If you are seeking clarity on a decision you need to make, you might choose a mantra such as "Enlighten my path," or, from Psalm 86, "Teach me, Lord, what you want me to do." From the Zuni peoples, "*Wah! Taho! Taho!*" (Rise! Arise! Arise!); from the Muslim tradition, "*La ilaha illa Allah*" (There is no god but God), "*Ihdinas Siratal Mustaqim*" (Show us the True Path), and "*Ishk Allah Mahbud Lillah*" (Allah is the Love, Lover, and Beloved).

If you come to your labyrinth walk without any particular need, allow the mantra to come to you during your preparation time. Sometimes while you are driving to your labyrinth or during your time of preparation, a word or phrase for that day's journey will make itself known to you. Be in a state of readiness for what comes to you from your subconscious self. Try not to edit what is given to you. You may be given the phrase that you need but are unaware of yet.

Again, the Psalms contain many passages that are appropriate to say during your journey.

> How I love your Temple, Lord Almighty!
> How I want to be there!
> I long to be in the Lord's Temple.
> —*Psalm 82:1–2*

> I was glad when they said unto me
> Let us go to the house of the Lord.
> —*Psalm 122:1*

Other biblical phrases work, too, such as "The spirit of God has made me, and the breath of the Almighty gives me life" (Job 33:4).

If you are part of a faith community with a prayer book, choose one of the opening sentences appropriate to the day and season. The opening words of the Episcopal *Book of Common Prayer* work well as prayers to be said as you walk the labyrinth; for example, the rite for daily morning prayer reads: "The glory of the Lord shall be revealed, and all flesh shall see it together." This prayer can be repeated over and over as a mantra or it can be the focus of your meditation.

Many faith traditions have canticles, chants, and responses that are sung. Choose one that is familiar to you and sing it as you make your labyrinth walk. Recorded music is also appropriate. However, music that is more chantlike—repetitious or without words—works better than music with complicated lyrics that may distract you. Many fine recordings of such music are available in the New Age section of your local music store.

Reaching the Center

When you reach the center of the labyrinth, take some time to experience the center before stepping out on the outward journey: sing there, dance there, or have intimate conversations with your friends. The center is also the perfect place to meditate. From the many different types of meditation, three are particularly helpful for your time at the center of the labyrinth: quiet meditation, guided meditation, and focused meditation.

Prayer and quiet meditation differ slightly from each other. If prayer is more like talking, then quiet meditation is more like listening. Quiet meditation is the awareness of the Spirit within our selves. It is the process of becoming conscious of that Spirit. Quiet meditation requires silence—no words, no music, no script. Quiet meditation is just being and/or walking in the silence. Quiet meditation is a kind of holy listening. From quiet meditation comes peace, improved health, inner joy, a spiritual dropping of the shoulders and unclenching of the fists.

Upon arriving in the center of your labyrinth, sit or lie down. Empty your mind of all thoughts. In most meditation practices, the goal is to empty one's mind of any thoughts. The reason for the emptying is to prepare a space and a place for the Holy. That makes a certain amount of sense: if we fill our lives up with clutter, there is very little space left for the Spirit.

Allow your body to relax into the center of the labyrinth. Be in the silence; let your *self* be silent. Do not try to think about anything. If thoughts float into your mind, allow them to float away. Do not dwell on any thought. If you are new to quiet meditation, do not chastise or berate yourself if inner quiet does not come right away. Like all spiritual disciplines, quiet meditation takes practice over many days, weeks, months, and even years. Newcomers to meditation may want to begin with either guided meditation or focused meditation.

In guided meditation, you are verbally guided into a meditative peaceful state of mind by someone else. If you will be walking with a group, each person can take a turn leading the meditation on different walks. If you will be walking alone, you may want to record your own guided meditation or have a friend record one for you. The latter is probably a better choice. Sometimes listening to one's own voice can be distracting. There are many guided meditations available on CD from spiritual or religious bookstores and catalogs. A word of caution about prerecorded guided meditations: Listen before you buy. There are some voices that you will find calming and peaceful, and there are some that you will find irritating. There is nothing worse than trying to calm yourself through guided meditation when the voice you are listening to causes you to get more and more agitated. Find a voice and a style of guiding that is pleasing to you. The ideal time duration is about twenty minutes. You will need to adjust the timing to fit your labyrinth walk. Walking a public labyrinth that has many visitors or walking a labyrinth that is outside and dependent on weather conditions will determine the length and style of guided meditation that works in that particular setting.

A focused meditation is different from the others. In a quiet meditation the ultimate experience is characterized by emptiness: one empties the mind of all thoughts. In focused meditation, the mind is filled with new insights and learning. In a focused meditation you may want to focus and gain insight from a selection from sacred texts or other holy writings—not in an intellectual way, but in a metaphorical or symbolic way, a right-brain experience rather than a left-brain one. Before starting on your journey, select a passage from a holy text, such as a psalm, and write it on a piece of paper. It is better to write the passage out and take it with you on your walk than to be encumbered with a book or be distracted by other words on the page. When you reach the center, read the passage several times. Put the passage away. Close your eyes. Let whatever words, images, smells, tastes, or feelings come to you at will. Try not to force the process. Allow the images or words to come to you; do not go after them. Be with the passage. Be the passage. The intent, as with all meditation practices, is to lead you to be still and to open you to spiritual gifts. Spend ten to fifteen minutes, if your situation allows, listening to and watching the images that come to you. Although this task may sound tedious, you may want to write out several passages all at once. Put each one on a separate 3 x 5 card. As you leave home to go for your walk, randomly select one of the cards. Do not read it until you are in the center of the labyrinth.

In some of the rituals described in the following chapters, there are suggestions for other objects of focus. You may want to start a collection of objects that you can take on your walk to help focus your meditation time. Put them in a basket near your door. Take one with you as you leave home to go to your labyrinth.

The Outward Journey: Walking the Labyrinth Out

When you are ready, begin the journey outward. Remember that the path out is of equal length to the path in. It is important to be as intentional about the outward journey as the inward journey. The genius of the labyrinth lies partly in the fact that the journey inward is the same as the journey outward—into the center *and* out into the world; not either/ or, but deliberately and intentionally both/and. As you take this outer journey, you may notice that your body feels lighter and more relaxed. You may experience a feeling of great joy or ecstasy. Do not be surprised if you feel taller and find yourself walking with more intention and integrity. As you take the journey back out into the world, imagine taking a gift to the world from the center of the labyrinth. The gift could be in the form of something you are going to do for the greater good, or an act of creativity like a song, poem, or piece of writing that you will share with the world. It does not have to be a tangible gift. You already are a gift that God has given to the world. By walking the labyrinth with intention, you will begin to recognize the gift that you already are. As you claim this recognition, the world will begin to change around you and because of you. Remember that every action and thought ripples and impacts on the whole of creation. Everything and everyone is interconnected. As you return to the world bringing the gift of the center and the gift of you back out into the world, be in a state of thankfulness and goodness. Take some time as you step out of the labyrinth to say a prayer of thanksgiving.

Thanksgiving: Expressing Gratitude for the Walk

Prayers of thanksgiving are really more than just saying "thank you." In the Bible, thanksgiving is upheld as a primary attitude toward life and God—a primary attitude, a way of living thankfully, a way of being in the world. Thanksgiving is an attitude toward our total experience as human beings. That means that we give thanks to God, who cares for us and for all people in the midst of whatever has happened, is happening, and will happen. Living in the state of thanksgiving is like being lost in the ecstasy of God. Living in a state of thanksgiving is like living your life as the great *yes*!

In the Jewish tradition there is a holy day that is celebrated as a time of thanksgiving called Sukkot. It is a festival marking the ingathering of the crops of the autumn harvest, as well as a remembrance of the dwelling in huts by the Jews during their wanderings through the desert after the Exodus. In the Torah, the Jewish people are told to take the fruit of a "goodly tree," traditionally a citron, and use it on the holy day of Sukkot. The citron is a member of the citrus family. For your prayer of thanksgiving, carry a citron with you to remind yourself as you walk to be in a perpetual state of thanksgiving. Citron is widely grown in India and may be available in some larger supermarkets that specialize in produce from around the world. Candied citron is easily found in most baking sections of your local grocery store. It is used to make fruitcakes and fruited breads. Walk the great *yes*! Be the great *yes*!

Reflecting on the Walk: Journal Writing

There are many techniques for journal writing. If you already journal your life's story, continue your practice. If you are not already journaling, you may want to start writing about your experience in and with the labyrinth. You may wish to set aside a special journal just for your labyrinth experiences. After each walk and journey, take some time to record your experience, either in total or in snippets, words, or pictures. You may find that one journey gives insight and texture to the ones that follow. You may discover that you are directed to explore variations on the labyrinth walk described in the rituals in the following chapters. Be gentle with yourself. Go well.

Making and walking a beach labyrinth.

SIX

Walks for Rites
of Passage

IT IS NO SECRET THAT LIVING A FULL LIFE ON EARTH IS a series of mountaintop and deep valley experiences. There is a tendency for humans to believe that if one is living a good life one should not have to experience any pain. However, that view is unrealistic: it is necessary to have highs and lows in order to grow and learn and live life to the fullest. Often, identical experiences can generate opposite feelings. When a loved one who has been ill for a long time dies, there are feelings of great loss, but there are also feelings of relief. If you believe in an afterlife, then feelings of joy are also appropriate. Earlier cultures celebrated natural passages in people's lives with rituals. Contemporary American culture is practically void of passage rituals. Except for the occasions of partnering, dying, and the occasional birthday party for children, rites of passage are almost nonexistent.

One reason for this decline in ritual celebrations is that we no longer live in villages, tribes, or clans. Our relatives live all over the world, and our friends come from a variety of faith traditions or from none at all. We may even be headed toward a time when the only community we know is the people with whom we interact via e-mail. The tribe or clan celebrated life passages with rituals and community gatherings. These rituals provided individuals as well as the larger community with opportunities to experience the full range of human emotion.

In the United States people are living in a conundrum. Religion has gotten in the way of spirituality, that connectedness to all things with a sense of wonder and awe. People are searching and seeking for a deep spiritual experience even as they are leaving organized religion, frustrated by its lack of depth and meaning for today's harried and hurried life. Returning to rituals that celebrate and honor life's passages can help to satisfy the deep longing that so many people have. In the suggestions for labyrinth rituals that follow, you will find some walks that are meant to be walked alone and some that are meant to be walked with others. Celebrating life's passages alone, with two or three friends, or with a larger group will bring meaning back into your life's journey. The labyrinth walk provides an opportunity for you to gather some friends and/or family and reintroduce rites of passage into your lives. You do not need to find thousands of people to accomplish this; two or three are enough. Some of the rituals require the kind of preparation that might be difficult to do in a public labyrinth. Feel free to adapt the ritual to your own needs, location, and climate. These rituals follow the order described in chapter 5: preparation, invocation, inward journey, center, outward journey, thanksgiving, and journal reflection. In order to make the labyrinth walk unique to a specific life passage or situation, try some of the suggestions that follow. Every ritual is not described in detail. If one or more of the elements of the ritual are not described, use suggestions for the general ritual found in chapter 7 or create your own. The possibilities are infinite. The following rituals are designed to spark your own creativity. Do not be afraid to use a mix-and-match approach. Some songs and prayers are appropriate to more than one occasion, and, when used in different passage rituals, open up for us nuances we may not have thought about when used in their traditional place.

Celebrating a Conception

This ritual is a celebration after a wanted conception has taken place. It is for both of the prospective parents to do together and is a ritual of hope and thanksgiving. Although only one of the prospective parents has conceived, both can image being pregnant with possibility and hope.

Preparation: Place a small bowl of seeds in the center of the labyrinth. If your location, season, and living space are appropriate, place a potted small tree in the center. You can plant the tree later in your yard at home.

Invocation: "Holy One, we stand in awe. You have blessed us, and we are not afraid. As we journey today, guide our path. Help us to make a place in our hearts for the new gift of life that you have given to us. So be it."

Inward Journey: Repeat the mantra "New life, new hope, new joy!"

Focused Meditation: Hold a seed carefully and gently. Focus your intention on the seed. Allow the seed to teach you the lesson that you need for the day.

Outward Journey: If you have placed a tree in the center, carry the tree with you on your outward journey. Repeat the mantra "New life, new hope, new joy!"

A Walk during Pregnancy

This ritual walk is a monthly walk for the mother-to-be to do alone or with her partner. Plan the walk to coincide with the one of the phases of the moon. During the first trimester, plan the walk for two or three days after the new moon. During the second trimester, walk on days when the moon is in the first quarter. During the last trimester, walk on days close to the full moon. Pray the invocation and mantra suggested in the conception ritual. If possible, time your labyrinth walk during the time of day when you will be able to see the moon. The moon will appear a day or so after the new moon as a tiny sliver in the west. Every day it will appear about an hour later, slightly higher in the sky. By the time of the first quarter, the moon will be overhead at sunset. As it approaches full, it will rise more and more in the eastern sky until it rises in the east at sunset on the day it is full. Focus your meditations during the first trimester on new beginnings and hope. During the second trimester, focus on the changes taking place in your body and watch how it is preparing to accommodate the new life you are carrying. During the third trimester, allow yourself quiet meditation time. Allow yourself to be in the intensity and tension of your pregnancy as your body prepares itself to burst forth with new life.

A Birth Ritual

This is a family ritual. On the first day of pleasant weather after the birth of the child, take the baby on its first labyrinth walk with its parents and any siblings. If your family includes grandparents or other close relatives, take them on the walk too. This is a quiet walk. Encourage all participants to walk and be in silence. One of the parents carries the baby on the inward journey, and the other carries the baby on the outward journey. If the siblings are young, include them by asking them to lead the way or to carry some flowers or some other symbol of joy and newness. They may have their own ideas about what to bring. Be in the awe and preciousness of the moment. A special family time of thanksgiving can be shared at the end of the walk.

Invocation: "Holy One, guide our path today as we celebrate the birth of our child. Grant that this first walk be the beginning of [his or her] life's journey with you. Bless [names of those present]. So be it."

A Rite for Naming a Child

There are two options for the naming ritual. One is to treat it as a family walk. Another is to envision it as a large community ritual. You may want to do both—experience the intimacy with the family and celebrate the joy with the large group.

A FAMILY NAMING RITUAL

Preparation: Prepare the labyrinth by placing a large candle (unlit), a basket, and a rose in the center. Each family member participating should have a few days to think about a symbol that he or she would like to give to the baby. The symbol should represent some wisdom or hope that the giver wants to share with the baby. Bring the symbols to the ritual.

Inward Journey: Enter the labyrinth in this order: baby first with a parent, the other parent, siblings, other relatives. Each person carries a symbol and reflects on it.

Naming: Hold the baby up, calling his or her name. Read the following scripture from the Jewish tradition, or find another more suited to your own religious tradition: "Do not be afraid, [child's name]—I will save you. I have called you by name—you are mine. When you pass through deep waters, I will be with you, your troubles will not overwhelm you. When you pass through fire, you will not be burned; the hard trials that come will not hurt you. For I am the Lord your God" (Isaiah 43:1–3). Light the candle. Have each person present his or her symbol, briefly explaining its meaning to the group. Put the symbols in the basket. One of the parents takes the rose and the basket.

Outward Journey: All repeat the mantra "Thank you for the precious gift of [child's name]."

A GROUP NAMING RITUAL

If you have not already performed the family naming ritual, place a candle and a rose in the center. Have all the guests stand in a circle outside the labyrinth. Only the parents, baby, and siblings will participate in the walk. As the family takes the inward journey, the guests and/or musicians can sing appropriate music. When the family reaches the center, light the candle. All should be in silence for a few minutes. Then one of the parents should stand facing east, holding the baby to the east, and say, "We present [baby's name] to the Spirits of the East. We ask that the Spirits of the East protect and guide [baby's name] on [his or her] journey through life. Keepers of the dawn, of thoughts and new beginnings, breathe on [baby's name], fill [him or her] with inspiration, and lead [him or her] to noble truths. So be it." Hold the baby to the south and say, "We present [baby's name] to the Spirits of the South. We ask that the Spirits of the South protect and guide [baby's name] on [his or her] journey through the hard times. Keepers of the midday sun, of fire and blood, spark in [baby's name] a desire for justice and lead [him or her] with courage and compassion against all oppressions. So be it." Hold the baby to the west and say, "We present [baby's name] to the Spirits of the West. We ask that the Spirits of the West protect and guide [baby's name] on [his or her] journey through life. Keepers of the setting sun, and all the waters that cover the earth, flow through [baby's name], like the moon's tides, bringing in treasures and taking out the dross of life. Forever replenish [him or her] with cool clear water. So be it." Hold the baby to the north and say, "We present [baby's name] to the Spirits of the North. We ask that the Spirits of the North protect and guide [baby's name] on [his or her] journey through life. Keepers of the tallest mountains and the deepest valleys, ground [baby's name] in this reality. May [he or she] know when to be as solid as rock and as malleable as clay. Keep [him or her] safe in your womblike caves. So be it." Hold the baby close to the earth, and say the following prayer, or adapt one to fit your own tradition: "YHVH God scooped up a handful of clay"—hold the baby up to the sky and say—"and breathed breath into *adam*. [Baby's name] created from the dust of the stars, we honor you."

Take the rose and begin the outward journey. Music may be sung again. You might want to start with soft music, gradually reaching a crescendo as the baby and family emerge from the labyrinth. Clapping, cheering, singing, dancing, and eating serve as the thanksgiving.

Honoring Puberty

Puberty rites in our society are virtually nonexistent. We have lost a very important ritual. The transition between childhood and adulthood is difficult even in the best of times. Not to honor and be conscious of the struggles and tensions inherent in this process exacerbates the strong and sometimes harsh feelings generated at this time for the adolescent as well as the parents. The young person needs to struggle against the parents, and the parents need to hold onto the offspring. To act this tension out in a safe way, through a ritual that honors the tension, helps families realize that what is happening is okay and is just part of the natural process of life. Family life in our society would be blessed if more families participated in puberty rites and rituals. We could learn something by revisiting some of the puberty rites of other cultures and times.

Before the ritual takes place, have the young person gather with a few selected friends. Tell them about the different parts of the ritual and what each part means. Guide them in designing their own ritual. Allow them the freedom and flexibility to be creative.

Some young people may be embarrassed having older people at their ritual. Encourage the young person to think about what this time in his or her life is about. Ask the young person to invite some older people whom he or she admires or considers important. Without being pushy, suggest to the young girls that they try to include a group of women of different ages in their ritual. For young boys, suggest a group of men of different ages. The young person may send a special invitation to the older persons.

Birthday Celebrations

Regardless of how old the birthday celebrant is, it is always appropriate to celebrate a birthday with balloons. A special labyrinth birthday walk can be made with the celebrant's birth mother if she is still alive. Some balloon suggestions:

- On the outer circumference of the circle, place as many helium-filled balloons as possible. Weight them down so they will not float away.
- In the inner circle, place a bunch of helium-filled balloons, enough so that each participant can carry one on the outward journey.
- Each participant carries a balloon on the inward journey and gives it to the birthday celebrant, who carries the bunch on the outward journey.

(Although it is incredibly tempting to let the balloons fly away, and the symbolism of the act of being set free is intriguing, do not let the balloons go if you are outside. The rubber of the balloons attracts birds and animals and they choke to death.)

Becoming Partners

Several days before the partnering ceremony, each partner should make his or her own private journey to the center of the labyrinth. In preparation, place a bowl of water in the center along with a white candle for purity and some purifying oil or incense. On the inward journey, reflect on your life up until this moment. Start with your earliest memories, and as you walk, gradually see yourself growing older. Allow the images to flow freely. Allow both the happy and sad memories to flow through you. At this moment you are the sum total of your life's experience. When you reach the center, light the candle, symbolically wash yourself, and anoint yourself with the oil of purity or burn the incense. Focus your meditation time thinking about your beloved. On the outward journey, allow dreams of your future together to flow through you. Write a prayer of thanksgiving that you might want to share with your partner.

Falling Apart:
A Walk for Times of Difficulty

There are times in our lives when it seems that everything is falling apart. Ritualize the feelings. As you take the inward journey, imagine in your mind's eye each part of your life that is falling apart. Metaphorically catch it and gently lay it on the path of the labyrinth. Allow it (or them) to fall. Instead of madly trying to keep it all together, just let the parts fall away. As you gently catch it (or them) and lower it to the path, thank it for falling away in order to give you some time to put yourself back together the way you want to be. During your meditation time, decide which things you are going to put back together and which things you are going to leave on the labyrinth path. On your outward journey, gently pick up those parts that you have decided to take with you and tuck them neatly into your imaginary backpack. Do not worry about those parts of you that you have left behind. They are safe in the labyrinth if you ever want to come back and retrieve them.

Commemorating Separations

Joinings and partings are the fabric of life. Imagine a macramé work of art. Sometimes the threads are knotted together; sometimes they are not. Different strands intimately knot and reknot with the same strands. Some never knot together, whereas others knot together once or twice, with each going its separate way never to meet again; so it is with life. Some people are life friends; others bless us only for an instant. Walk the labyrinth with the one from whom you are about to be separated. As you walk, reflect on how the labyrinth path brings you close together at times and takes you far apart at other times. Notice that sometimes you will meet face-to-face and at other times go in the same direction. Sometimes it feels as if you will never find each other again, and then you are united in the center. When you reach the center, share with each other stories of your time together. Tell each other what gift the other has been to you and your life. Allow yourselves time to laugh and cry. After the outward journey, give thanks that this person has been part of your life and your journey.

Healing Rituals

Each person's life journey is that person's journey. It is presumptuous to decide for others that they should be healed if they are sick, that they should stop suffering if they are suffering, or that they should live if they want to die. How each person lives life, travels the journey, or faces dying is that person's responsibility, and each of us is ultimately in charge of our own decision about whether or not we want to participate in a healing ritual. If a person wants to regain his or her health, others can assist in the process. If a person wants to let go of the present life for the next life, others can offer support for that decision.

If you choose to participate in a healing ritual, there are some caveats to keep in mind. First, it is not our responsibility to make another person well or to try to prevent them from dying. We can only be channels of healing love. Whether a person lives or dies is up to that person and their God. Second, it is important to keep one's ego out of the way. If the person does heal, we should not take credit for it but simply be thankful that we were able to assist in the healing process. Praying with a person for bodily healing does not always bring about physical recovery. Sometimes the healing happens in ways we do not expect. Even though the physical body does not appear to be healed immediately, healing has taken place. Do not forget this.

There are many different healing techniques: Jesus used the laying on of hands; in early Judaism it was common to anoint people with oil; modern healers like Bernie Segal use visualizations; and contemporary doctors use chemicals and machinery. Each method has its pluses and minuses. The method you use is up to you and the person asking for the healing.

Preparation: Place a chair in the middle of the labyrinth. Gather two or three friends who are comfortable and want to participate in the laying on of hands. Light some patchouli, sandalwood, or champa incense (for healing) and a green candle (for life) for each of the healers and a white candle (for purity) for the person asking for the healing.

Invocation: One person carries the incense around the outside of the labyrinth while the others say, "Make me a channel of your love."

Inward Journey and *Outward Journey:* Walk the labyrinth with the person asking for healing in the middle of the line. Carry the lighted candles. Repeat the mantra "Heal and protect us."

Center: Place the candles around the circumference of the inner circle. Have the person requesting healing sit in the chair. Before touching the person seeking healing, ask for permission to touch them. If the person does not want to be touched, the ones who are channeling should place their hands three to five inches from the person's body. If touch is okay, place your hands on the person. Be sure to be in a comfortable position. Have one of the participants read or say the following guided meditation. Use a soft, comforting tone of voice. Invite all to close their eyes and relax.

> Imagine all the pain and hurt in your body flowing out of you like a river, flowing out through your feet into the earth. Allow the earth to absorb all the pain. Do not be afraid to let go of whatever is causing your body to be at dis-ease. Imagine the light of God's healing filling you. Imagine God's love surrounding you. Feel the warmth of that love. Feel the tingling sensations in your body as you are cleansed and filled with that love. Imagine being whole and well. Imagine God's holy light surrounding you and lifting you up. Imagine God's love filling you and making you lighter and lighter. Allow God's love to swirl around you and flow through you. [Silence for several minutes.] So be it.

A Menopause Walk

Gather some women of different ages. Premenopausal women should make a circle around the outside of the labyrinth.

Postmenopausal women should enter the labyrinth according to age, oldest first. The one to be honored should enter the labyrinth when most of the postmenopausal women are at least halfway to the center. Each of the older women should present the one being honored with a token gift. One gift could be a crown that the newly honored one wears on the outward journey. Poems, artwork, and music are appropriate.

Celebrating Retirement

Gather your friends and relatives for a retirement party. At some time before the ritual begins, the retiree should take the inward journey and wait in the center. When it is time, have the guests gather in a circle outside the labyrinth. The retiree makes the outward walk. Much celebration should happen when the retiree steps out of the labyrinth.

A Walk for Healing from a Miscarriage or an Abortion

This ritual is for women who have had a miscarriage or an abortion. Do this ritual with a very small group of female friends. In preparation, before leaving home to go to the labyrinth, take a warm bath. Use some herbs of comfort and healing in the water, like lavender. Sprinkle the bath with rose petals. After the bath, take the rose petals out of the water. Take a cup of the bathwater to the labyrinth; it represents your birthing waters that were not able to come to fruition. (If your labyrinth is indoors, you will also need a bowl into which you can pour the water.) Invite one of your friends to walk around the outside of the labyrinth, calling forth all angels and guides to be present and to protect the women who are present, the labyrinth, and the ritual. Have one or two of your friends precede you and one or two of your friends follow you as you make the inward and outward journeys.

Center: If possible, lie down in the center of the labyrinth with your friends, heads in the center, feet toward the outside, like spokes of a wheel. Close your eyes. Ask your friends to lead you in the grieving process by making moaning and wailing sounds. Let the sound reach to heaven. If you are in an outdoor labyrinth, when the wailing has ceased take the water and pour it into the ground. If you are in an indoor labyrinth, pour it into a bowl and later pour it into the ground. The earth will take the water and transform it for the greater good by nourishing plants. Take the petals and throw them into the air. Say (or sing) aloud, "And God will lift us up on eagle's wings, bear us on the breath of dawn, make us shine like the sun, and hold us in the palm of God's hand" (from *The Methodist Hymnal,* No. 143).

Outward Journey: Repeat the mantra "I am held in God's hands."

A Walk for Dealing with a Hysterectomy

Having a hysterectomy can generate very different feelings, depending upon the age of the woman experiencing it. For women younger than forty, the hysterectomy can generate incredible feelings of loss: of womanhood, of potential children, of sense of self. For women who are postmenopausal, there are still feelings of loss and of assaults on the body, but there may also be some feelings of relief. A ritual is appropriate both before and after the operation.

Do the preoperation ritual as near to the time of the operation as possible. Gather a few close female friends.

Invocation: "Holy One, the soul of woman, some say, is found within her womb—the nest of flesh unborn. But where is woman, then, if by chance the womb is lost? Surely her soul is not also lost! There must be a way to say, 'O woman, may your empty space be filled with the light of God.' Holy Spirit, create within her now a nest of love to nurture and prepare the woman's spirit to be reborn. So be it."

Processing the Death of a Loved One

When someone dies, we wonder how God could do such a thing. We forget that death is part of life. We are angry with God. The feelings of anger toward God are especially strong when the person who died is a son or a daughter, a parent, or a partner. It is okay to be angry. It is okay to be angry with God. It is okay to scream and shout and throw a tantrum. Being angry is part of the grieving process—a necessary part that cannot be denied. Many of us have grown up in a society that tells us not to cry. In an attempt to shield us from sorrow and grief, funeral directors cover the earth at the gravesite with plastic grass. Except in Jewish tradition, it is very rare to be allowed to stay at the grave when the coffin is lowered into the ground. Whenever someone we love dies, we have to grieve. Other cultures have something to teach us about dying and about grieving. In some cultures, there are women who have the specific responsibility of mourning. They cry and wail and make moaning sounds. The women lead the others in the grieving process. When you walk the labyrinth after the death of a loved one, use the meditation time to grieve by making moaning sounds, allowing your whole body to cry and wail. You may want to devote one of your monthly walks to grieving. Honor your body's need to have some time to experience the deep sadness resulting from the loss of a loved one. The closer the relationship, the longer the grieving process; do not hurry it. Allow yourself to visit the labyrinth at least monthly for a year with the only intention being to walk through the grief.

Preparation: Place mementos of your loved one who has died in the center of the labyrinth with white candles and flowers.

Inward Journey: Try one of the following, or something similar from your own religious tradition:

- Repeat the mantra "The Lord God will wipe away the tears from every cheek" (Isaiah 25:1–10).
- Repeat the mantra "God, I am coming to you" (John 17:11).
- Reflect on "Show me the way in which I should walk" or "Make me to know your ways, O God" (Psalm 25:4).
- Reflect on "God is my refuge and strength, a very present help in trouble" (Psalm 46:2).
- Allow yourself to remember your life and the life of your loved one and how they blessed each other. Allow the tears to flow.

Meditation: Allow yourself to weep by holding the mementos of your loved one. Say good-bye.

Outward Journey: Walk in silence or sing a song or hymn that is your favorite or the favorite of your loved one.

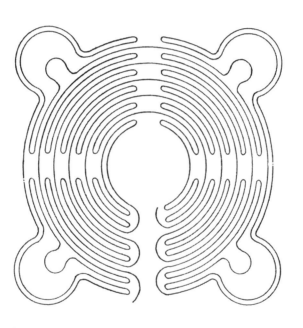

A Minnesota labyrinth in winter and summer.

SEVEN

Walks for the
Four Seasons

MAKING CALENDARS AND CELEBRATING HOLY DAYS
are activities every culture has participated in since the first
people looked up to the sky and noticed the sun, moon,
and stars. Over the eons, religious calendars and holy days
changed into secular calendars that regulate business and
commerce, and holy days became holidays so workers could
have a day off to play or be with their families without guilt.
Seasons have had a series of names, changing to match the
favorite gods of whoever was in power at the time. The present calendar, though starting with a date that more or less
coincides with the birth of Jesus, still marks its months and
days by honoring other gods and celestial bodies.

Dates that designated the first day of the new year varied
from culture to culture. Whatever the names, or dates, some
things remained constant, seasonal calendars evolved to help
humans stay in touch with the rhythms of nature, and rituals
evolved to help the people celebrate their holy days.

There is a paradox about rituals. On the one hand, fa-
miliarity—the repetition of the same words and actions at
the same time every year—contributes to a sense of transcendence, like the repetition of a mantra. On the other
hand, repeating the same ritual may cause some seekers to
become bored and may make the rituals seem like empty
words with no meaning, creating a "been there, done that"
attitude. There is a fine line between transcendence and
boredom. Somewhere there is the right balance for you—
a repetition of familiar words and actions that makes you
feel comfortable yet remains unique enough to shed light on
your life and spiritual journey in new ways. With their peri-
odic recurrence, seasonal rituals may help you to find your
right balance. Doing a new ritual every time you walk the
labyrinth may cause you to worry rather than to sink into
the substance of meaning. Seasonal rituals offer a solution,
regardless of whether they are based on cosmic astronomical or traditional religious liturgical events. Try one of the
seasonal rituals for several months before switching to a different one. Each of the seasonal rituals has the same format
throughout the year, with minor changes to coincide with the
seasonal variations. The modification might be as simple as
changing the color of the candles with each season. The Four
Seasons Ritual changes four times per year, the Celtic Ritual
changes eight times, the Zodiac Ritual changes twelve times,
and the Moon Ritual changes thirteen times. The number of
celebrations in the traditional religious year varies according to the specific religion. However, many major religions
have celebrations and festivals occurring about the same
time. This happens partly because many of the world's major religions base their festival dates on astronomical events
like full moons and on seasonal changes like the first day of
spring. Therefore, many of the metaphors and symbols are
interchangeable.

For each seasonal ritual, the basic format is the same throughout the year, with suggestions for metaphoric and symbolic changes to heighten and deepen the seasonal meanings. You may discover that it helps to keep one aspect of the ritual the same throughout the year, such as always praying or singing the same thanksgiving prayer regardless of the season.

Colors are important in bringing meaning to our lives because they speak to the nonlogical part of us. We already associate colors with different holidays and holy days. Red and green mean Christmas, pastel yellows and purples make us think of spring, orange and black generate images of Halloween, and red, white, and blue remind us of American holidays. The same is true for symbols. Even a modern artist's rendition of an evergreen tree sparks warm feelings of the Christmas season; the cross reminds one of Christianity, and the Star of David reminds one of Judaism. Many earth-centered religious traditions also identify specific colors and symbols with their seasons. The Christian church has designated different colors and symbols for each season. The colors and symbols vary among the different traditions, but that does not matter. What matters is that the symbols and colors mean something to you. The colors and symbols associated with any of the different seasonal rituals can easily be adapted to your labyrinth walk to both heighten and deepen your journey.

The incredible wisdom of symbols is that they encompass the whole and speak to the seeker in ways that words cannot express. Symbols not only hold the opposites for us—like yin and yang, light and dark, positive and negative, the crucifixion and the resurrection—but also an infinite number of subtleties of meaning. Plumbing the depths of all aspects of a symbol helps to bring meaning into our lives. In any ritual, symbols, metaphors, and regalia contribute to the total experience.

Part of walking the labyrinth is intentionality—walking with intention. Walking the labyrinth is not just going on a stroll, it is a conscious intention of walking purposely on your spiritual journey. Being on a spiritual journey invites the seeker to pay more attention to symbols and metaphors in order to bring deeper meaning into one's life. Part of the malaise of the current American culture is that it is bereft of spiritual symbols and meaning. We have lost touch with even the simple changes of the earth's seasons. We live in climate-controlled buildings and drive in climate-controlled vehicles. We speed to and from work in cars, buses, planes, and trains and miss the flowering bushes and trees of spring and the fiery treat of the autumn colors.

All the rituals described here can be modified to adjust to your labyrinth location. Some rituals suit outdoor labyrinths while others are for indoor ones. Some rituals are better for a solitary walk, others for groups.

The Four Seasons Ritual

If you do not have a religious tradition or if you are unfamiliar with particular seasonal rituals, the simplest seasonal ritual to follow on your labyrinth walk is the Four Seasons Ritual. The Four Seasons Ritual follows the same format suggested earlier: preparation, invocation, inward journey, center, outward journey, thanksgiving, and journal reflection. If you walk daily or weekly, the Four Seasons Ritual will help you attune to the natural cycles of the earth as it travels around the sun.

The seasons are more clearly identifiable as you travel farther away from the equator. These seasons happen because the earth is tilted on its axis. If one drew a line between the poles of the earth, and if this line were perpendicular to the plane of the earth's path around the sun, life on earth would be a different experience—or maybe there would be no life at all. If you live in the southern hemisphere, adjust the colors and symbols to match your environment. If you live in tropical climates, where extreme seasonal changes are not so obvious, you may want to try the Four Seasons Ritual to help you get a new perspective on the earth's cycles.

The four seasons, four directions, and four ancient metaphorical elements of fire, water, earth, and air overlap. The following ritual contains aspects of all of them. If you are already familiar with an earth-honoring ritual, continue your practice, adjusting it to any of the following suggestions.

SPRING

Spring marks the beginning of things. The element for spring is air and things of the air. It is appropriate to focus on the animals of the air—birds and flying insects—wind, flying, light airy flute music, intuition and creativity. Do not be afraid to include all aspects of the air, especially hurricanes and tornadoes. Allow your imagination to play with the images of air in all its forms and colloquial uses: "Blow me away"; "You could have knocked me over with a feather." From the Jewish and Christian traditions, there are endless images associated with air: "Breath of God," "Ruach," "Holy Spirit," "Suddenly there was a noise from the sky which sounded like a strong wind blowing, and it filled the whole house where they were sitting" (Acts 2:2). Choose light pastel colors like pinks and yellows—the colors that remind you of a spring sunrise—for clothes or other adornments.

SUMMER

Summer is the time of the high energy of the middle of things. The element for summer is fire and things of fire. It is appropriate to focus on animals that are big and strong, like lions, tigers, or dragons; wild hot music, Beethoven, or hot jazz. Remember volcanoes and hot flowing lava, campfires and forest fires, stars and supernovae. From slang there are phrases like "light my fire" and "burning desire." From the Bible, we have images of the burning bush and "Then they saw what looked like tongues of fire, which spread out and touched each person there" (Acts 2:3). Choose colors that remind you of fire—reds and dark oranges—for clothes or other adornments.

FALL

Fall marks the end of things—the end of the day, sunset, and finishing up. The element for fall is water and things of the water. It is appropriate to focus on animals of the sea, like whales, fish, and dolphins. Do not forget the crabs, sharks, and octopuses. Use soothing music like chant. Remember water in all its forms, gentle rains as well as floods and tsunamis. Many popular songs have some form of water in the title or lyrics, such as "Singing in the Rain" or "Moon River." In Jewish and Christian scriptures we find the story of Noah's ark and the flood as well as baptism. Choose colors to reflect the deep dark blue and green of the ocean for clothes and adornments.

WINTER

Winter is the time of introspection, reflection, and rest. The element for winter is earth—dirt and stones and things of the earth. Reflect on trees and plants and the nourishment that comes from the soil. Allow your imagination to explore caves and high mountain peaks. Do not forget earthquakes and landslides. It is appropriate to focus on animals in hibernation, like bears, or creatures that live in the earth, like moles, worms, and snakes. Select drums and music with a heavy driving beat. Remember hymns like "Rock of Ages" and popular songs like "Love Me Like a Rock." From the Jewish scriptures we read about a pillar of salt (Lot's wife) and the tablets of the Ten Commandments. Winter is a time of not doing, of incubating, of resting deep in the earth like tulip and daffodil bulbs. Choose earthy colors of dark browns and golds for clothing or adornment.

Preparation: On the outer circumference and within the center circle of the labyrinth, place the following items: toward the east, incense; toward the south, burning candles; toward the west, water; and toward the north, a stone or bowl of soil. On the outside of the labyrinth, also place a ribbon or a long, thin piece of cloth like a stole: pink or yellow in the east, red in the south, blue in the west, and brown or gold in the north.

Start the ritual standing in the appropriate direction for the season. If you are doing this ritual in the spring, stand in the east, wear the pink stole, and pick up the incense. For summer, stand in the south, wear the red stole, and carry the candle. For fall, stand in the west, wear the blue or green stole, and carry the water. In winter, start in the north, wear the dark brown or gold stole, and carry the stone or bowl of dirt. Standing in the appropriate direction, face away from the labyrinth and invoke the spirit(s) appropriate to the season or invoke the spirit of one of the animals associated with the season. Some religious traditions have animal spirits already designated for each of the four directions: eagle in the east, coyote in the south, grizzly bear in the west, and white buffalo in the north. If you are uncomfortable invoking animal spirits, invoke the spirits of angels, gods, or goddesses.

Invocation: Say or sing one of the following invocations appropriate to the season or use the suggestions above to create your own prayer or song of invocation.

Spring: "Spirits of the East and of the springtime, I call upon you to be present with me today as I take this walk into the center of my soul. Beginning of beginnings, begin again with me. I call upon the birds of the air to give wing to my burdens. Carry them away to a safe place, so that later I may lift them one by one and repack them in a more manageable way. I call upon the butterflies of the air to guide my thoughts and meditations, to create in me the holy space where my spirit may grow safely and then birth into new life. So be it."

Or, "Hail to you, Spirits of the East and of the sky. God[dess] of all beginnings! Come and be present at our rite as I [we] perform according to your sacred ways. Send your holy wind to purify me [us] that I [we] may walk forever in perfect love and perfect trust." You can also use a hymn or song appropriate to your own tradition.

Summer: "Spirits of the South and of the summertime, I call upon you to be present with me today as I take this walk into the center of my soul. Burning heat of compassion, a tiny flicker bursting into flame, fill me with energy. I call upon the lions and tigers of the south to give me strength and courage to take the steps I need to bring about justice where I see injustice. Ancient dragons' spirits, baptize me anew with the fire of love and passion. Protect the holy space within me, where my spirit grows and is bursting into flower. So be it."

Or, "Hail to you, Spirits of the South and of the fire. God[dess] of all passion and compassion! Come and be present at our rite as I [we] perform according to your sacred ways. Send your holy fire to purify me [us] that I [we] may walk forever in perfect love and perfect trust." You can also use a hymn from your own or another tradition.

Autumn: "Spirits of the West and of the autumn, I call upon you to be present with me today as I take this walk into the center of my soul. I call upon the creatures of the flowing waters, the fishes and playful dolphins, to carry my forgotten dreams and lost hopes into the deep, deep stillness, where they may be renewed in the birthing waters. Powerful floods and raging rivers, wash over me like a gentle cleansing rain.

Great whales, carry me deeper and deeper into the oceans of the holy space within me so that I may conceive my dreams again. So be it."

Or, "Hail to you, Spirits of the West and of the water. God[dess] of all endings! Come and be present at our rite as I [we] perform according to your sacred ways. Send your holy water to purify me [us] that I [we] may walk forever in perfect love and perfect trust."

Winter: "Spirits of the North and of the wintertime, I call upon you to be present with me today as I take this walk into the center of my soul. Ground me again. Gentle earth, quake within me. Shake loose the crust that has protected me thus far. O spirit of Mother earth, rock me gently in your silence. I call upon all the creatures that crawl upon the earth. Great snakes, symbols of life, rejuvenate my spirit power. Guide my thoughts and meditations; create in me the holy space where new life may prepare to birth forth. So be it."

Or, "Hail to you, Spirits of the North and of the earth. God[dess] of all rest! Come and be present at our rite as I [we] perform according to your sacred ways. Transform me [us] in your soil so that I [we] may walk forever in perfect love and perfect trust."

Before starting the inward journey, carry the symbol of the season slowly around the labyrinth in a clockwise direction. Carry the symbol of the season with you on your inward journey.

Inward Journey, Meditation, and *Outward Journey:* Choose prayers, mantras, meditations, and visual imagery appropriate to the season or your personal need. For example, during spring, reflect on air or on your breath. You may want to try pondering the negative or destructive aspects of wind or air, like hurricanes or air pollution, or on someone with asthma or emphysema on the inward journey. During the meditation time, imagine the transformation of the destructive nature of wind to the positive.

As you make the outward journey, think about positive aspects of air, such as God breathing life into the first human, or sailing—or just focus and pay attention to your breathing.

When returning to the outside of the labyrinth, still carrying the symbol of the season, slowly walk counterclockwise at least once around the labyrinth and back to the starting point. Thank the spirits of that direction for their help, protection, and guidance. Replace the symbol and stole. Take a few minutes to write in your journal about the insights and gifts that you received on each day's labyrinth walk.

Walking a labyrinth indoors.

EIGHT

Walks in Many Spiritual Traditions

MOST SPIRITUAL TRADITIONS HAVE A YEARLY CYCLE OF celebrations and festivals. Before the advent of the modern age, priests and leaders of these religions set holy days on or near some astronomical event. It was easy to identify when the moon was full or when a certain constellation appeared in the east. This helped the people to keep track of and know when to expect certain celebrations. Consequently, many of the world religions celebrate their holy days at the same time. Later, many secular celebrations became associated with the same times. For example, Groundhog Day, the day thought to determine the length of the North American winter, is at the same time as the cross-quarter day of the Celtic calendar, Lupercalia, and St. Brigit's Day or Candlemas in the Christian calendar. Among rituals, celebrations, and festivals, there are many similarities in world religions. Most of the religions have a day of remembrance: for Christians, it is All Saint's

Day; for Jews, one day of remembrance is Yom HaShoah; for witches, it is Halloween.

Many of the ancient and modern world religions originating in the northern hemisphere have holidays in December. For example, the date of the birth of Jesus was superimposed on the winter solstice celebration. In the northern hemisphere on the day of the winter solstice, the sun rises as late as it ever rises and sets as early as it ever sets. Primitive people may have feared that the days would continue to get shorter and shorter and eventually the light would be gone forever. Every year the people experienced the solstice as a miracle, as the light slowly started to increase. In some mythologies, the light won out over the darkness. The people created great festivals to celebrate this triumph of the light over the dark. When the leaders of the Christian Church were searching for a date for the birth of Jesus, they chose the time of year when the people were already celebrating the coming of the light into the world. Many of the songs and hymns and much of the Christian symbolism refer to Jesus as the light of the world, the one who came in the darkness of winter. Other religions also have holy days celebrating light: Chanukah, in the Jewish tradition; Kwanzaa, in the African American community; the Festival of Lanterns, in Japan and China; and Diwali, in parts of India.

The following suggestions for holy day labyrinth walks are not meant to be exhaustive of all the holy days celebrated by all the world's spiritual traditions—that would require another book. The background and ritual suggestions are meant to help readers from strong religious backgrounds as well as no religious background to rediscover and reclaim new meaning from the vast possibilities that already exist. The symbolic and metaphoric meaning for most holy days can be adapted easily into a labyrinth walk. Some of the rituals that require certain sacred objects that cannot be moved from their holy place are difficult to replicate in a labyrinth; for example, it would be difficult to take Torah scrolls out of the ark for labyrinth use. However, it is always appropriate to walk the labyrinth either in preparation or in thanksgiving for your particular holy day celebration.

In many of the world's spiritual traditions, the clerical leaders wear special garments for the different holy days. In some cases, the colors chosen symbolically reflect the meaning of the celebration. For example, the symbolic color of each season of the Christian year can be seen in the regalia of the church and clergy. For Christians walking the labyrinth, care might be taken to follow in the symbolic tradition of the church. This can be achieved by wearing some article of clothing to match the color of the season. For rituals involving candles, choosing candles of the appropriate color also contributes to the overall ambiance and mood.

Except for New Year's celebrations, the following rituals are grouped more or less by season: winter, spring, summer, and fall. The dates for many traditional religious holy days are determined by the date of the full moon. This causes the actual calendar date to vary greatly from year to year. Much of the symbolism and metaphoric meaning connected with these traditional rituals are similar to the suggestions previously mentioned for seasonal rituals and those mentioned in the following chapter on the Celtic year and the zodiac. Feel free to mix and match from the various sections of this chapter to create rituals unique to your own holy day.

New Year's Celebrations

Most of the world religions celebrate the beginning of things or at least the beginning of a new year. The actual day of the new year or cycle varies around the world and from culture to culture. In Vietnam and China, the new year begins on the first day of the lunar calendar, sometime between January 21 and February 19. Jews celebrate new beginnings around the autumn equinox with Rosh Hashanah and Yom Kippur. For Hindus, there are four new year celebrations, one for the turn of each season.

The current secular calendar of Europe and North America started with the Romans. Julius Caesar moved the beginning of the new year from March (when the zodiac year begins) to January in honor of the god Janus Befors. Janus Befors had two faces, one that looked back and one that looked forward. The idea of looking backward and forward lends itself to walking the labyrinth. On the inward journey, reflect on the past, on the outward journey look to the future.

ADVENT (FOUR SUNDAYS BEFORE CHRISTMAS)

For Christians, the year starts with Advent. The season of Advent is a time pregnant with hope and expectation, a time of preparation. As the days get shorter and shorter throughout December, the need for hope increases. Historically, the color for Advent is purple, the color of penitence and introspection. Recently, the color has changed to blue in the more liturgical Christian churches, like the Roman Catholic Church. Blue is the color of hope and anticipation. There are four Sundays in Advent, each with its own symbolism and ritual. The Sundays represent hope, peace, love, and joy. While there is a traditional order, use the order that meets your specific tradition or need. On the third Sunday, the color changes to rose pink. In some traditions, the third Sunday of Advent was also called *Gaudete* Sunday, a Latin word meaning "rejoice."

For the Sundays in Advent, you will need three purple or blue candles and one rose-pink candle. Designate a focus word for each Sunday—for example, hope on the first Sunday, followed by peace, love, and joy, on each following

Sunday. If you are a practicing Christian, follow the pattern used in your local congregation. Many churches offer Advent meditations to their parishioners. If you have an Advent wreath, place it in the center of the labyrinth before you start the ritual. Light one blue or purple candle before you begin your walk. Depending on where your labyrinth is, this ritual will have more impact if it is done in the evening or in a darkened room. Walking toward the light of the one candle will bring new meaning to the words "The people who walked in darkness have seen a great light; those who lived in a land of deep darkness—on them light has shined" (Isaiah 9:2). On the second Sunday of Advent, light two candles. Continue in this way, adding a candle each Sunday until all four are burning brightly. As the days get shorter and the nights get longer, the flames of the candles will seem to get brighter and brighter.

ROSH HASHANAH

For Jews, Rosh Hashanah is believed to be the birthday of the world. It begins on the first day of the month of Tishre, and its date is determined by the new moon. It falls sometime between early September and early October. As part of the traditional Rosh Hashanah ritual, Jews are encouraged to walk to a body of water, such as a river or a lake, to perform the ceremony of Tashlikh—to symbolically cast or throw one's sins away in the form of bread crumbs. Rosh Hashanah is a time for genuine soul-searching and of letting go. For your labyrinth walk on this day, wear white. In preparation, place some pieces of apple, a small container of honey, and a bowl of water in the center of the labyrinth. Carry a few bread crumbs with you. In preparation, read Genesis 22:1–19. On the inward journey, reflect on the past year. This is not a time to be morbid, but it is a time to reflect on how you acted during the past year. Upon reaching

the center, recite Micah 7:19: "The Eternal will have compassion upon us; the Eternal will subdue our iniquities. And
you will cast all their sins into the depths of the sea." Throw
the crumbs into the water. Dip the apple into the honey, and
reflect on the hope for the new year. Say, "May it be God's
will to grant us a good and a sweet year." On the outward
journey, allow yourself to reflect on the sweetness of the
coming new year.

NO-RUZ (MARCH 21)

In Iran, the new year begins on March 21 and lasts for thirteen
days; it is known as No-Ruz. During No-Ruz, people often
eat candy or something sweet while passages of the Qur'an
are being read. This represents the belief that people should
be happy when the new year arrives. Symbols appropriate
for carrying on your labyrinth walk are green sprouts grown
from seed, hyacinths, sweet wheat pudding, vinegar, sumac,
apples, or olives. In the center of the labyrinth, place colored
eggs, a mirror, and a candle for each person participating in
the ritual.

HOLI

Holi is celebrated the day after the full moon in early March
in India. Originally, Holi was the celebration of a good harvest. Today it is a celebration of a Hindu legend in which
Prince Prahlad escapes from burning in a huge fire. On the
eve of Holi, the people light great bonfires. The celebration
of Holi is one of colorful exuberance and joy. In Vrindavan
and Mathura, India, the celebration lasts at least sixteen days.
Here the festival is associated with the love of the incarnation
of the god Krishna and his lover, Radha. People sing, dance,
and march in processions.

For your labyrinth walk on Holi, prepare yourself and
your labyrinth with bright colors, streamers, flowers, and

other colorful banners. The walk for this day is not somber in any way but is one of pure abandonment.

YUAN SHAW

The Festival of Lanterns, or Yuan Shaw, is celebrated on the first full moon after the Chinese New Year. Do this labyrinth walk in the evening under the full moon. Place lanterns around the perimeter of the labyrinth.

Winter

CHRISTMAS (DECEMBER 25)

The Christmas season begins at sundown on December 24 and lasts until January 5–6, a period commonly known as the Twelve Days of Christmas. Following are two rituals, one for Christmas Eve and one for the twelve days of Christmas. The color for the season is white.

Christmas Eve Ritual: This ritual is better done alone. If you belong to a group, or if you walk a public labyrinth, try to arrange the timing so that you are able to be alone for this walk. Women can imagine themselves as Mary, and men can imagine themselves as Joseph. If it helps to get into character, the women could wear a shawl draped over their heads and the men could carry a staff or walking stick. As you walk the path, pretend that you are walking to Bethlehem. Imagine that you are about to give birth to a new part of yourself. This is a metaphorical birth—so men can imagine giving birth also. Do not push the process; it takes nine long months to birth a child. Allow yourself all the time you need to birth a new you or a new part of you. When you reach the center, sit for a while; imagine holding and nurturing and tending this newborn you. When you are ready, gently and carefully imagine taking this new creation out into the world.

The Twelve Days of Christmas Ritual: The twelve days of Christmas are probably best known through the song of the same name: "On the first day of Christmas my true love gave to me...." On each day, for twelve days beginning with Christmas, symbolically carry a gift on your labyrinth walk. The symbol could be a picture of a Mercedes-Benz, or some other material item, but in keeping with the spirit of the Christian season you might select something less tangible and perhaps more meaningful, like "caring." On a piece of paper write the word, or draw a symbol representing the word to you. On your inward journey, think of this gift as a gift to yourself—for example, caring for yourself. On the outward journey, think of this gift as a gift for another, such as caring for a friend or a group of people, like refugees. Be creative and take your needs, life, and world into consideration—for example, good health, loving relationships, fun, joy, bliss, peace, and/or meaningful work.

KWANZAA (DECEMBER 26–JANUARY 1)

Kwanzaa is a relatively new celebration, started in 1977 by Dr. Maulana Karenga, but its roots are as ancient as the African continent. Kwanzaa is celebrated for seven days, each of which symbolizes a principle: *Umoja*, unity; *Kujichangulia*, self-determination; *Ujima*, collective work and responsibility; *Ujamaa*, cooperative economics; *Nia*, purpose; *Kuumba*, creativity; *Imani*, faith. Kwanzaa is the time when families and friends gather to celebrate African-American culture and traditions.

In preparation for the walk, place a candleholder of seven candles in the center of the labyrinth—three red candles on one side, a black one in the center, and three green ones on the other side. If you plan to walk each day of Kwanzaa, light one candle each day representing each of the seven principles. As you walk, reflect on the principle for that day. If you are planning a small community event, seven people can each light one of the candles.

EPIPHANY (JANUARY 6)

The Epiphany season begins on January 7, the day after the feast, and lasts for a variable number of weeks (from four to nine, depending on the date of Easter), ending on Shrove Tuesday, the day before Ash Wednesday. Epiphany is the metaphoric day that the magi, the wise men, arrived in Bethlehem. Light and stars are used to symbolize the cosmic nature of the birth of the Christ. The color for Epiphany day is white, whereas the rest of the season is green, symbolizing growth. During the Epiphany season, Christians around the world hear stories of Jesus' ministry and the calling of the apostles. During Epiphany, focus on listening to God's call to you as you take the inward path to the center. During the outward journey, focus your thoughts on how you are going to be in the world on that day or in that week. If you happen to be in the process of one of life's passages (chapter 6) use the Epiphany season to shed light on your passage. For example, if you are considering a job change, hold the new job in your mind's eye as you journey into the center of the labyrinth. You may want to hold it as an offering or a gift. After some reflection time in the center, you may decide to leave the new job there, possibly symbolizing that this is not right for you at this time. On the other hand, you may find that this new job is exactly right for you, so you can symbolically take this new job back out with you into the world.

Shrove Tuesday (Mardi Gras or "Fat Tuesday") marks the end of the Epiphany season. This is a good day to invite your friends to a party and labyrinth walk. In the days when many more Christians fasted or did not eat meat during Lent, the people had to eat up the meat and fat that was in their larders at this time so that food would not be wasted. The wearing of costumes and the great festivities associated with Mardi Gras represent a kind of last hurrah before the quiet introspection of Lent. In the earliest centuries of Christianity, Lent was a time of preparation for those who would be baptized into the Christian faith at Easter. In later centuries Lent became a season of fasting and austerity. Since the Second Vatican Council (1962–1965), the emphasis of Lent in the Catholic Church has shifted to preparation for Easter, not only for new initiates but for all Christians.

Spring

LENT

In Old English, *lent* means "spring." Christians use the period as a time of preparation before the feast of Easter. For most Christians, Lent starts with Ash Wednesday and lasts for forty days, including six Sundays. The color is purple, for penitence. The focus during Lent is on the inward journey. The forty days of Lent mirror the length of time Jesus prayed in the wilderness before he started his ministry. During his wilderness experience, Jesus struggled with his temptations. He listened to the quiet, he listened to the angels, and he listened to the animal spirits for guidance. For your labyrinth walk during Lent, focus on the temptations in your life that may be keeping you from finding your true self. Carry them into the center and leave them there. As you make the inward journey, allow your body to droop or slump, bow your head, and look down. Walk as if carrying a heavy burden. In your mind's eye, or in pantomime, take off your burden and leave it in the center of the labyrinth. Change your posture on your outward journey. Feel lighter, pull your shoulders back, lift up your head, look ahead or up, and smile. Depending on the nature of your burden or temptation, you may have to repeat the process several times throughout the season.

HOLY WEEK

During Holy Week, Christians commemorate the final events of Jesus' life. It begins with Palm, or Passion, Sunday a week before Easter and lasts through Good Friday, two days before Easter. The color of Holy Week is a dark, blood red, representing the low point on the Christian path, ending with black on Friday. If fasting is a good spiritual practice for you, you might consider a modified fast during Holy Week. Holy Week, like the twelve days of Christmas, lends itself to a daily walk, if that is possible for you. To capture the mood of Holy Week, remember that the week starts with a community parade and ends with capital punishment. Make a large cross about four feet high and three feet wide. Styrofoam, stiff corrugated cardboard, or quarter-inch plywood works fine. Think of a person who has died needlessly, like a political prisoner, a victim of domestic violence or of a drunk driver, or a person with AIDS. Print the person's name on the cross in large letters. Every day throughout Holy Week, carry the cross to the center of the labyrinth. You may choose to take a different cross on the journey every day for the week, but be sure to remove the crosses before Saturday evening.

EASTER—THE RESURRECTION OF CHRIST

For those living in the northern hemisphere, Easter's symbolism of new life and rebirth can be concretely experienced in the earth's dramatic transformation in the spring. The colors for Easter are traditionally white and gold. Easter is a high celebration of joy and awe. The death, despair, and desolation of Holy Week break forth in the celebration to end all celebrations. Easter is the ultimate manifestation of God's love for creation. It falls on the first Sunday after the first full moon after the vernal equinox.

Easter Ritual: Depending on the weather, try sleeping in the center of the labyrinth starting sometime late Saturday night. Even if it is not cold, use a sleeping bag. If you cannot sleep in the labyrinth overnight, go to the labyrinth before the sun rises and lie in the middle of the labyrinth in your sleeping bag. Imagine being in a cocoon. Pull the sleeping bag over your head for the full effect. Just as the sun (son) rises, slowly begin to shed your cocoon. When you are rebirthed and ready, joyously journey out of the labyrinth.

THE EASTER SEASON

The Easter season begins with Easter Sunday and lasts for fifty days. Easter rituals are more conducive to morning walks. If your schedule allows, making the labyrinth walk early in the day on the days of the Easter season, just when the sun (son) is rising, helps to capture the meaning of resurrection and new life in Christ.

PASSOVER

There are three major themes for the celebration of Passover, or Pesach, which occurs sometime between late March and late April: the Exodus of the Jews from Egyptian slavery after the ten plagues; the Festival of the Unleavened Bread, an early agricultural festival celebrating the beginning of the barley harvest; and a feast marking the season in which lambs were born. Liberation from all kinds of bondage is the essence of this holiday.

For a variation on a walk for Passover, walk through every room in the house where Passover is being celebrated. All participants can follow in a snakelike fashion, or each individual can walk the rooms separately. The size of the room and arrangement of furniture, of course, will determine how much walking can be done in each room. If possible, walk in the doorway of each room, circling the perimeter of the room, slowly spiraling into the center and out again, continuing into the next room. Arrive in the room where the Passover seder is to be held. As you spiral through each room, remember the items on the seder plate. *Charoset*, a mixture of apples, nuts, wine, and spices, symbolizes the mortar the Jewish slaves made in their building for the Egyptians. *Zeroa*, a shankbone, is a reminder of the "mighty arm of God" and also the lamb offered as the sacrifice in Temple days. *Baytzah*, a hard-boiled egg, symbolizes the days of the Temple or the mourning for the loss of the two Temples (the first was destroyed by the Babylonians in 586 BCE, the second by the Romans in 70 CE). *Karpas* is a vegetable (celery or onion), parsley, or potato that is dipped in salt water, which represents tears. *Maror* is bitter herbs—horseradish root or prepared horseradish—which represent the bitter life of the Israelites during the time of their enslavement in Egypt. *Chazeret* is a bitter vegetable, usually romaine lettuce.

SHAVUOT

Shavuot is a Jewish celebration held seven weeks after Passover, near the end of spring. It marks the wheat harvest and is sometimes called the Festival of Firstfruits. It is also the anniversary of the giving of the Torah at Mount Sinai. During the synagogue ritual, the Torah is carried around the congregation, symbolizing that the Torah belongs to every Jew, regardless of class, status, or education. If you are walking the labyrinth, place a representation of the Torah in the center of the labyrinth. Carry the Torah out of the labyrinth, symbolizing the bringing of the Torah down from Mount Sinai.

THE BIRTH OF THE BUDDHA (APRIL 8)

This holiday is celebrated in Japan, where it is called Hana Matsuri, as well as in other countries where Buddhism has flourished. It is a festival of flowers. It is also the day that people travel to the temple to bathe the Buddha in sweet tea made from hydrangea leaves. Prepare the labyrinth with many flowers. In the center, place a replica of the Buddha and a small bowl of herb tea. On the inward journey, carry flowers to place in the center. Upon arriving in the center of the labyrinth, gently and reverently pour the tea over the statue of the Buddha.

Summer

PENTECOST

Fifty days after Easter is Pentecost, the day when Christians celebrate the descent of the Holy Spirit upon Jesus' disciples. Pentecost is a fiery time. It was a day in the Christian story when flames of fire were seen coming out of the tops of the heads of the assembled gathering. It is the day to adorn yourself in red—bright, fire red. This is the day to allow the Holy Spirit to set you on fire, to fire you up, to ignite a spark in you. Come to the labyrinth walk on this day prepared to have the Holy Spirit burst your heart open to infinite possibility. For your walk you may want to use the mantra "With God, all is possible."

Prepare the labyrinth with a fire in the center. If you are outside, you may actually have a small fire. If inside, you can use a large metal container, cauldron, or bucket filled with sand and many candles. Light the fire or candles before you begin your walk, so that you are walking toward the fire. Have enough red tapers for each of the participants so that upon arriving from the inward walk, each person can light a candle to symbolize being set on fire by the Spirit. Take the fire (candle) with you as you return into the world.

PENTECOST SEASON

The Pentecost season lasts several months, from sometime in May to sometime at the end of November, depending on the date of Easter. In the Roman Catholic Church, this season is referred to as Ordinary Time. For the Church, this is the season to celebrate the spirit's growth, both individually and collectively. For labyrinth walkers it may be the season to focus on the ordinary things of life like the rituals of passage in chapter 6. Pentecost may also be the time to walk with the angels, gods, and goddesses.

Most Christian denominations have prayers, songs, books of worship, and hymnals filled with resources for each season. While books are convenient, they are also cumbersome. It is difficult to light candles, find pages in books, and do other "housekeeping" activities without getting caught up in the mechanics. Even though symbols contribute to the overall experience, keep the objects of the ritual to a minimum. For example, even though it may take some extra time at home, copy the prayer or hymn that you want to use on a particular day onto a piece of paper. It is easier to tuck a piece of paper somewhere, up a sleeve or in your waistband, than it is to figure out what to do with the book.

OTHER SUMMER FESTIVALS

During the summer, all manner of fairs, carnivals, and festivals take place around the world. Let your imagination create a new labyrinth ritual to include singing, dancing, and games of many kinds. After the labyrinth walk, plan to celebrate with food and music and many friends.

Fall

THANKSGIVING

Almost every religion has some form of harvest celebration, a time to be thankful for the bounty of the land. In the United States, the harvest celebration is a national holiday participated in by many faiths. In many communities, Thanksgiving is celebrated with ecumenical services. Because endings are also beginnings, many of the world's religions have New Year celebrations on or near festivals of the harvest, several of which have already been mentioned. For a labyrinth walk celebrating the harvest, see Lammas in the section that follows.

Making a labyrinth on canvas.

A stone labyrinth in Pennsylvania.

NINE

Walks for the Celtic Year and the Zodiac

IN RECENT YEARS, SOME SPIRITUAL GROUPS HAVE RE-claimed a calendar that celebrates the movement of the sun throughout the year. While some claim this calendar as Celtic, other religious and cultural groups around the world celebrate the same days, but give them different names. The astronomical events are known the world over and, it appears, were noted by celebrations of ancient peoples. Many modern-day Wicca groups have also claimed these holy days.

The sun appears to travel around the sky through certain constellations on a path called the ecliptic. The constellations on the ecliptic became known as the zodiac. Every year since time immemorial, the sun has been in the same constellation and at virtually the same point in the sky on the same day each year. There is some slippage, known as the precession of the equinoxes, but it is not discernable for many generations. It takes about two thousand years for the point on the ecliptic where the sun crosses the equator on the vernal equinox to move from one zodiac constellation to another. Thus, the vernal equinox is not final at 0 degrees Aries (the point used by astrologers) but is actually now in Pisces.

The ancients noticed that the sun appeared to be in the same constellation at the same time each year. For those living in the northern hemisphere, the sun is as close to the horizon as it will ever get on the day of the winter solstice. People made great celebrations on this day. It meant that the sun would again start to bring back more minutes of light and warmth per day in the northern hemisphere.

The ancients identified eight points on the sun's path across the sky: the winter and summer solstices; the spring and autumn equinoxes, and four cross-quarter days.

The winter and summer solstices mark the sun's lowest and highest point on the ecliptic, respectively. The two equinoxes are halfway between the solstices, when sunrise and sunset are exactly twelve hours apart. The four cross-quarter days occur halfway between each solstice and equinox, thus dividing the ecliptic in eight parts. Each of these eight days has its unique celebrations, symbols, metaphors, and rituals.

It does not matter where you live on the planet; these eight points are the same. The symbolism around light and dark change depending on whether you are in the northern or southern hemisphere. The dramatic effect of what appears to be the sun leaving or returning is not as noticeable if one lives between the Tropic of Cancer and the Tropic of Capricorn.

Some groups celebrate their New Year's Day on the vernal equinox, which coincides with the beginning of the zodiac year. Some groups begin the New Year on the winter solstice, because it nearly coincides with Christmas and the end of darkness and the coming again of the light. Some groups, like Wiccans, celebrate the New Year on the cross-quarter day between the autumn equinox and the winter solstice, known as Halloween. The Christian church's birthday, Pentecost, is celebrated near the cross-quarter day between the vernal equinox and the summer solstice, known as Beltane.

All beginnings are also endings, and all endings are beginnings. In a circle, it does not matter where you start, because you will eventually come back to the same place. Begin your New Year on one of the days that has meaning for you. Each of the eight days has many names because so many different cultures and spiritual groups find these eight days important in bringing meaning to their lives. The same is true for the variety of rituals that have come to be associated with these holy days. The following list is only a sample of the possibilities that exist and is not meant to be exhaustive. Feel free to bring your own symbols, rituals, and cultural history to the celebrations. A detailed ritual follows for Halloween. Suggestions for the other seven holy days are given to help you design your own rituals.

Halloween (October 31)

Halloween is the cross-quarter day between the autumn equinox and the winter solstice. It is also called All Hallow's Eve and is believed to be the time of the year when the barrier between this life and the next is the thinnest. The wearing of costumes of ghosts and skeletons represents the idea that the spirits of those who have died can easily slip back across the barrier between life and death. Once a year the souls of the departed are allowed to come back for the evening.

Many popular traditions have evolved over the centuries around Halloween. The Christian church named the day after Halloween "All Saints' Day," in keeping with the tradition of remembering the dead. In Celtic tradition, this day is known as Ancestor Night, the Feast of the Dead, or Samhain. Dedicate this labyrinth walk to your ancestors.

Preparation: Find a guided meditation that takes you to a place where you are allowed to spend some time with a Wise One, or record the one suggested in the Center section of this ritual. Light black tapers in the center of the labyrinth, one for each of your friends or immediate family members who have died during the past year. Light a large black pillar candle for all your other ancestors. You will also need a token offering that you will bring to the center: a cracker, a piece of cake, or a small jar of water or wine. These will be left in the center. If you are walking an indoor public labyrinth, you will have to leave symbolic gifts for the ancestors or else take your gifts out with you when you leave. If you must do it this way, you may want to leave your offerings for your ancestors by a tree or some other location on your way home from the labyrinth. You will also need one white candle for your walk. Light it just before you begin the invocation.

Invocation: "O Spirits of my departed ones, I have come to honor you. Come to me on the whisperings of the wind. Help me to remember that you and I are connected through time and history, blood and genes. I am part of you. You are part of me. All those who wish me well are welcome on my walk tonight. So be it."

Inward Journey: Carry the lighted white candle with you as you walk. Remember those who have gone before you. Upon arriving at the center, make your offering to your ancestors. Wish them well. Ask for their continued guidance.

Center: Allow yourself to go on a guided visualization. (Pre-record the following guided meditation and play it for yourself.)

> Close your eyes; become aware of your breath. With each breath you inhale, allow the light of the universe (God, Spirit) to fill your body. With each breath you exhale, allow the tensions, pains, and hurts to flow into Mother Earth, where they will become fertilizer for your growth.

Continue to follow your breath. Allow yourself to walk up a gently sloping hillside. Smell the flowers and the trees. Listen to the birds and the insects. Feel a gentle breeze on your face and in your hair. As you slowly climb the hill, notice up ahead that there is a bench overlooking the valley. Slowly climb toward the bench. As you get closer, you notice that there is someone sitting on the bench. Allow your disappointment to float away. Allow any fears you have to float away. The Old One sees you and beckons you to come and sit on the bench. You feel safe. You know that the Old One is here to be your guide on this night. Allow yourself to sit on the bench. Allow yourself to ask the Old One questions or to just have a conversation. (Spend about ten minutes with the Old One.) Allow the Old One to give you a gift. Now it is time to return. Thank the Old One for spending time with you. Slowly allow yourself to go back down the hill and back into the labyrinth. When you are ready, open your eyes.

Outward Journey: Carry the metaphorical gift that the Old One gave you back into the world.

Thanksgiving: Thank all the ancestors that were present with you on tonight's walk. Thank the Old One for the gift. Take some time to journal and reflect.

Winter Solstice (December 20–21)

On the winter solstice in the northern hemisphere, the sun is closer to the horizon at noontime than at any other time of the year. Holidays associated with this period have many names, including Yule, Alban Arthuan, Lucina, Chanukah, and Christmas. This is a wonderful time of year to borrow pieces of tradition from many cultures. The very air is filled with symbolism and metaphor. Explore your own cultural or family traditions. Identify one or two symbols and bring them into the light of your new consciousness. Find out everything you can about one of these symbols. Make the symbols real and your own. Carry the symbol on your spiritual walk; meditate on it. For those connected to the Christian path, try the Christmas rituals suggested in the previous chapter. Enhance one of the following suggestions with your own ideas.

If you are able, place votive candles around the circumference of the inner and outer circles of the labyrinth.

Walk the labyrinth in the darkest part of the night; walk the inward journey in the darkness. Meditate on the idea that tomorrow there will be more light in the world. Tomorrow you will be more light in the world. Carry a lighted candle, torch, or flashlight on the outward journey. Allow yourself to be a child again. Give yourself a gift.

Put a Christmas tree in the center of your labyrinth. Gather some friends to walk the walk singing favorite carols.

Gather a group to do circle dances around the outside of the labyrinth.

Candlemas (February 2)

Halfway between the winter solstice and the vernal equinox is the cross-quarter day known as Imbolc, Brigantia, Candlemas, Aradia, St. Brigit's Day, and Groundhog Day. This day is a time of initiation and spring cleaning, a time of purification, a time to set your inner and outer house in order, a time to start seedlings, a time to start thinking about beginning new projects. Think of the bulbs and seeds getting ready to push through the earth. For Christians, the season of Lent begins around this time.

Brigit was the triple goddess of the Celtic empire of Brigantia. Brigit was made a saint because the Christian church could not turn the people away from worshiping her. In Rome, the same day was celebrated as Lupercalia, a day honoring Venus. Lupercalia evolved into the Feast of the Purification of the Virgin and Candlemas.

Purification Ritual: In the center of the labyrinth put a bowl of water, a bowl of dirt, a lighted candle, and some burning incense. As you take the inward journey, symbolically remove or let go of any burdens that you are carrying. Take a few steps, stop, and imagine putting aside something that is weighing you down. Do not force the process. Allow the thoughts and images to come into your mind. Often our subconscious helps with this process by allowing burdens to surface that we have chosen to ignore. Do not dwell on them. Try not to edit them. Just let them float into your mind and then consciously put them aside. When you reach the center, say a purifying prayer as you cleanse yourself with water, incense, dirt, and fire. As you walk the outward journey, symbolically take up *one* (only one) of the burdens that you left along the path. If you choose, you may retrieve others on other walks. Do not overburden yourself. Take this one burden home for reflection and contemplation. Thank the Spirit for the opportunity of reflecting in depth on one of your burdens.

Spring Equinox (March 20–21)

On the spring equinox, the amount of light and dark is equal. For the Celts, it is called Alban Eiler. For Christians, it is the season of dying and resurrection that Easter symbolizes. For others, it is the time of newness. The northern hemisphere is turning green after the darkness of winter. Robins are seen in New England. The hibernating animals wake from their winter's sleep. In the fields and forests, females of many species give birth.

This is a good time to invite your friends for a labyrinth walk. For your ritual during this time, light green candles symbolizing life, one for each person present. Adorn yourself and your labyrinth with flowers. In preparation, place some little cakes and some new wine in the center of the labyrinth for your joy. The walk on this day is joyous, almost a skipping and dancing walk. This is a good day to listen to music or to sing as you walk. When you arrive in the center, share the cakes and wine. Enjoy each other's company.

Beltane (May 1)

Beltane is the cross-quarter day between the spring equinox and the summer solstice and is also known as Lady Day or May Day. For Christians, this day is close to the date of Pentecost. It is a time associated with fertility and mating. Continuing and amplifying the emotions of the spring equinox, Beltane moves us further into feelings of high hopes and anticipations, energy, dancing, singing, and a sense that all is well.

For this ritual, use lots of bright colors and streamers, like the ribbons of a maypole dance, colorful candles, and many flowers. Create an ambiance of good cheer and well-being. This is a joyous time. Sing and dance your labyrinth walk.

Summer Solstice (June 20–21)

The summer solstice, Litha, or Alban Heruin is the height of energy. For those in the northern hemisphere, this day marks the point in the noonday sky where the sun is as high above the horizon as it will ever get. The candles are red; the feeling is passion and compassion, almost out-of-control energy. Find a group of people who like to drum, or buy a recording of drumming. Start the drumming softly. Gradually intensify the volume as you walk toward the center. When the group enters the center, the drumming should be approaching fever pitch. Reverse the process as you take the outward walk. This can be a powerful and breathtaking experience. When you finish the walk, allow some quiet time to be in a state of thanksgiving.

Lammas (August 1)

Lammas is the cross-quarter day between the summer solstice and the autumn equinox, the beginning of the harvest season, known as Lughnassadh and Lunasa. The fields are full of the fruits of the earth. The focus of this ritual and the one for the autumn equinox is that of thanksgiving. The earth is giving us life in the form of fruits and vegetables for our health and joy. Take a basket of whatever fruits and vegetables have grown in your area and put them in the center of the labyrinth. Save one piece to carry on your inward journey. As you walk, feel it, smell it, look at it. Hold it gently and carefully in your hand and give thanks. Upon arriving in the center, meditate on each item or some of the items in the basket. Be in a state of thankfulness. Take one of the pieces and slowly, very slowly, eat it, truly experiencing each bite. Relish the juice as it runs down your face. Allow your taste buds to experience every little nuance of this piece of fruit. Identify its sweetness, its tartness, its uniqueness, and give thanks. Thank the fruit for its nourishment. Thank the earth for her bounty. Take the basket as you walk the outward journey. Deliver the basket to a friend or a homeless shelter or give it to a street person.

Autumn Equinox (September 22–23)

The autumn equinox is also known as Mabon and Alban Elved. This is the day to celebrate the return of the darkness; it is a time of slowing down, of getting ready to burrow into the earth. Unfortunately, the school year dictates our returning to the hustle and bustle of things. We have lost touch with our need to wind down, to replenish, to rejuvenate. We are always gearing up, with very few opportunities to rest and revitalize. Even our vacations are times of high energy and excitement. Take some time during this ritual to identify ways you can give yourself a rest. Let this walk be slow and calming with no tasks, no thoughts, no agendas. Sit peacefully in quiet meditation. If possible, take a nap in the center. Walk out as slowly as you can. Labor Day should really be celebrated on the autumn equinox—a time to rest from the harvest, a time to rest from our labors. Give yourself permission to take today or tomorrow off from your work. Do not do any errands. Just slowly walk the labyrinth and rest.

Zodiac Walks

Circles and cycles are common symbols throughout history. Different cultures around the world and in different eras have developed their own symbol system and set of rituals. While the names for the symbols have changed over time, some archetypal meanings are consistent and recurring. Humans have always given meaning to seasonal changes, acts of nature, and the movement of the sun, moon, planets, and stars. With our advanced knowledge of science and with the rapid growth of computer technology, we tend to dismiss the ancient ways as superstitious and primitive. Instead of dismissing these ancient spiritual practices as ridiculous, we should let the ancient ways shed some meaning on our frantic and out-of-touch lives.

One of the calendar-centered spiritual practice models is astrology. Some of the symbolism inherent in astrology can have meaning for us beyond the common practice of fortune telling. Daily newspaper horoscopes have done damage to the underlying metaphorical symbol system that is the basis for astrology. The famous astronomers of the early scientific era were astrologers, as these two fields were at that time still one.

If nothing else, studying some aspects of astrology connects us again to the heavens and reminds us of the cycles of our lives. The ancients noticed, after many years of watching the skies, that the sun, moon, and some stars (really planets) followed the same path around the sky, known as the ecliptic. The ancients also realized that there were twelve constellations on this path. Knowing when the sun was "in" one of these constellations helped the ancients to predict when it was time for planting and harvesting, when rivers would flood, or when it was time to move to summer or winter lodgings. These twelve constellations, known as the zodiac, acted like a sky calendar. Naming the constellations Aries, Taurus, Gemini, and so on, is no different than naming our months January, February, March, and so forth. In fact, our current month names are related to the ancient zodiac names. March, for example, was named after the planet Mars, which is the planet that "rules" (i.e., has an affinity with) Aries.

The names of the zodiac constellations were described with pictures so that the people could identify certain groups of stars. As with other calendar symbols, knowing what day or month it is lends meaning to one's life. For many in New England, May is the favorite month because it represents new life. The trees and shrubs are bursting with new flowers and leaves, the colors are soft and gentle, and breezes are warm on one's face.

Using the symbols and metaphors of the zodiac rituals can bring new meaning to your labyrinth walk. As with all symbols and metaphors, the zodiac constellations carry for the seeker qualities that can be described in many ways. Just as water is necessary for human life, it is also destructive. Fire can warm us and cook food, but it can also burn and destroy.

The zodiac constellations are archetypal symbols that carry human qualities, and these qualities can be manifested in either positive or negative ways. For example, a person may be perceived as stubborn by some or persevering by others, or a person may be stubborn in some cases and persevering in others. The quality is the same; the manifestation of the quality is different. The ancients attributed different aspects of the human condition to the twelve constellations of the zodiac. They told stories that were passed down from generation to generation to help them remember what these qualities are and how, with consciousness, one could make choices about one's behavior.

You do not need to know how to cast an astrological chart or even go very deep into an interest in astrology to use these archetypal images for bringing about personal growth. For the labyrinth walk, it does not matter when your birthday is. Just because you were born on March 22, for example, does not mean that you have only the qualities of an Aries. In fact, we all have some of the characteristics of each sign. To shed light on your own spiritual journey, focus on one of the qualities of each sign during its month. For example, when you walk the labyrinth between March 21 and April 20, focus your attention on the qualities suggested below for Aries.

The purpose of these zodiac rituals is transformation, not fortune telling. These rituals are primarily for those seeking personal growth and spiritual enlightenment. Below you will find a simple list of some of the qualities associated with the signs of the zodiac that have come down to us through the ages.

Preparation: Each sign of the zodiac is associated with one of the four elements. For walks during Aries, Leo, and Sagittarius, which are the fire signs, place a small fire in the center of the labyrinth. A simple transportable fire can be achieved by using a small metal container filled with sand and several votive candles. For walks during the earth signs of Taurus, Virgo, and Capricorn, place a small container of dirt in the center of the labyrinth. For walks during the air signs of Gemini, Libra, and Aquarius, place burning incense or a smudge pot in the center of the labyrinth. For walks during the water signs of Cancer, Scorpio, and Pisces, place a bowl of water in the center of the labyrinth.

On a tiny slip of paper, write a negative aspect of a quality associated with the sign that you would like to transform in yourself. On a second tiny slip of paper, write the positive, transformed quality. Place the second slip of paper under or near the bowl listed above.

Invocation: This or any invocation that supports and guides transformation and change in the seeker is appropriate. "Creative Life Force, I come today as I am, full of doubts and hopes, burdens and gifts. Be my companion on my walk today. Transform _____ into _____. (Select appropriate characteristics from the suggestions for each sign.) So be it."

Inward Journey: Carry the slip of paper upon which you wrote the negative characteristic as you walk toward the center. Allow memories and thoughts about how you have been and are like that quality to float into your consciousness. Do not dwell on it (them). Allow it (them) to float away as you walk.

Meditation: When you have reached the center, take the slip of paper with the negative quality and burn it, bury it, drown it, or let it float away into the air, depending on what element is in the center of the labyrinth. Sit in silence as you allow the transformation to take place in you. When you are ready, take the slip of paper symbolizing the transformed quality and read it several times before starting your outward journey.

Outward Journey: Carry the slip of paper with the transformed quality with you as you make your way back into the world. Think about how you are going to be like this transformed quality in the coming days.

TRANSFORMATIONS

Aries: March 21–April 20

From selfish and quick-tempered to dynamic and quick-witted

From impulsive and impatient to adventurous and energetic

From foolhardy and daredevil to pioneering and courageous

Taurus: April 21–May 20

From resentful and inflexible to persistent and determined

From jealous and possessive to warmhearted and loving

From self-indulgent and greedy to placid and security-loving

Gemini: May 21–June 20

From cunning and inquisitive to youthful and lively

From superficial and inconsistent to adaptable and versatile

From nervous and tense to communicative and witty

Cancer: June 21–July 22

From overemotional and touchy to emotional and loving

From clingy and unable to let go to protective and sympathetic

From changeable and moody to intuitive and imaginative

Leo: July 23–August 22

From dogmatic and intolerant to broad-minded and expansive

From pompous and patronizing to generous and warmhearted

From bossy and interfering to creative and enthusiastic

Virgo: August 23–September 22

From fussy and worrying to meticulous and reliable

From overcritical and harsh to practical and diligent

From perfectionist and conservative to modest and shy

Libra: September 23–October 22

From indecisive and changeable to idealistic and peaceable

From flirtatious and self-indulgent to romantic and charming

From gullible and easily influenced to easygoing and sociable

Scorpio: October 22–November 21

From secretive and obstinate to exciting and magnetic

From jealous and resentful to determined and forceful

From compulsive and obsessive to powerful and passionate

Sagittarius: November 22–December 21

From blindly optimistic and careless to optimistic and freedom-loving

From tactless and restless to honest and straightforward

From irresponsible and superficial to jovial and good-humored

Capricorn: December 22–January 19

> From miserly and grudging to practical and prudent
>
> From overly conventional and rigid to patient and careful
>
> From pessimistic and fatalistic to humorous and disciplined

Aquarius: January 20–February 18

> From intractable and contrary to original and inventive
>
> From perverse and unpredictable to independent and intellectual
>
> From unemotional and detached to friendly and humanitarian

Pisces: February 19–March 20

> From escapist and idealistic to selfless and unworldly
>
> From secretive and vague to imaginative and sensitive
>
> From weak-willed and easily led to intuitive and sympathetic

Moon Rituals

The moon also lends itself to seasonal rituals. The metaphor of waxing and waning, new moon and full moon are easily adapted to the labyrinth walk. Buy a moon calendar. Design your rituals to match the daily or weekly changes of the moon. Rituals emphasizing the positive qualities of both the light and the dark are appropriate. Depending on your taste and desire, plan to walk in the evening, just after sunset if you want to experience the beauty of the first sliver of light following the new moon. Walk at midnight if you want to experience being bathed in the light of the full moon. If your labyrinth is in a safe environment, there is nothing quite like the thrill of walking in the moonlight at midnight.

You may want to walk only at the times of the full moon. There are thirteen full moons in the course of the calendar year. The moon's fullness comes very regularly, every twenty-eight days. Different societies, cultures, and religious groups have given different names to the thirteen moons. If you walk the labyrinth only on the full moon, keep your ritual the same each month. If you want to add variety, there are many books available on moon rituals in your local spiritual or religious bookstore. Many of these will spark your imagination and creativity.

Epilogue

Labyrinths from the Inside Out

DONNA SCHAPER

WALKING AROUND IN PATTERNED CIRCLES CAN BE good for the soul. It can be good for the fruits, or consequences, of one's life: inner health gives outer capacity. However, some people get stuck inside, and they prefer to stay there. Some people internalize, believing that the inner or internal life is the only life. One of the most important messages of the labyrinth is the combination of the inward and outward journeys; they are the same path. I feel cheated if I cannot walk both in and out of the labyrinth on the same walk. Going in releases the energy for going out.

I was friends with a couple who had never visited the labyrinth in our backyard before. They went in and they went out with a kind of ease and normality of passage that was deeply moving. Some people who walk in, or coil, do not walk out, or uncoil. They just go to the center and sit and then leave, walking across the paths rather than along the path. Walking the outward path strengthens us for our life in the world. If we believe that a transformation happens in the center, then we need to bring the transformed self back into the world.

It is tempting to stay in the safety of the center, but if we care about participating in the creation of a new heaven and a new earth, if we care about being part of the creation of a better world, a world of peace and justice, then the outward journey is as important as the inner one. Walking the labyrinth helps us to find our way home: to the center and to our place in the world.

I met a girl on the Bosnian border in 1994. She was eleven years old. In her pocket were crumbs, turned green with mold, of the bread her mother had given her when she sent the girl out on her bicycle to find food. It was common then for children to travel hundreds of miles with inadequate maps, searching for what little food there was. The child was lost. She also spoke an unusual dialect, so it was nearly impossible to understand her. This girl was trembling. My job was to sit with her while an interpreter was found. No one came. Finally, through sign language, the child was put in touch with a Red Cross worker and was taken to England, where no doubt she still lives, a lost refugee, one of the literally millions whom God will eventually (we hope) save. As the girl put her hand into the hand of the Red Cross worker, she took the green crumbs out of her pocket and put them on the ground behind her. She coiled and uncoiled; she walked out of an old life and into a new life. Whenever I walk the labyrinth, I think of her and how my life links to her life. She took a long journey, and the journey took her to a new kind of home, a sure home. She is one of many people for whom the circle back home is to a new home. We uncoil: we move out into the world.

There are many people who are lost—many who are also last and least. These people are walking the labyrinths of the streets to get home; they are carrying their luggage on their backs in a real journey.

In the killing fields of Cambodia's Tol Slent, twenty thousand people were killed. One-quarter of the population of the country died. All the temples were destroyed and used as torture chambers. Interestingly, many Buddhist activists now walk the killing fields. They rewalk them to claim the land back from the deadly deeds that were done there. These circlings back remind me of the labyrinth journey. It is a spiritual action on behalf of a hoped-for reality—a metaphor for the time surely to come. The exiles will all get home.

We walk the labyrinth to enforce and reinforce our optimism. We do not walk it thinking that *we* will be able to save the exiles, the lost children, or the one I call "Green Bread." We walk it to remember what our hope is for them.

Some people, of course, will abuse the ancient circle for their own purposes. They are not evil as much as deprived of the full glory of the circle. Many have taken the kind of freedom that Dostoyevsky's grand inquisitor gave. By cheating people out of their humanity and offering them security instead, the grand inquisitor gave people a limited life in exchange for a loss of fear. Such people do not live as much as exist. The true meaning of the labyrinth is a scary freedom and good bread, not the cheap bread of the traded freedom. We walk to a place we do not know—and it is home.

In the base communities, the grassroots Christian groups of Latin America, sacred vocation is clear and urgent: to participate in the transformation of ourselves, our neighbors, and the world with all of its complexities. To do this we must practice our freedom. We must practice the promise. We are in real danger as a people. There are genuine threats to our ability to get back home. Our air and water are polluted. Global warming, all scientists now agree, is real. That girl in Bosnia was simply experiencing what many of us may yet experience. We need a counterorientation, a reorientation, a kind of simultaneous circling back and forward as implied by the labyrinth.

A labyrinth—whether it is cut into a field of sunflowers, taped onto a nursing home dining room floor, or made of mosaic tiles set into the floor of a great cathedral—follows an order ordained in early times. The living labyrinths, those made of flowers like the Sunflower Labyrinth at Annie's Garden Center, also obey the pattern of seasons—first green shoots, then rising stalks; then heads bursting with color, bent from riches of seeds, yet turning with the light. Then the flowers are cut back, leaving stiff silvery stalks. Their tops pave the path. Flower heads are patterned with empty seed pods, each step on a whorl, each whorl progressing from the center. Moving along the path, one can imagine being a fish in a stream, quietly following the currents and eddies, or a bird on an invisible migratory path, or a dolphin in some mysterious sea. One becomes a soul fixed on a journey, from the world, to the center, into the world.

Labyrinths will not solve our economic or ecological problems, but they will give us the strength to return to the center of ourselves so that we can go back to the task of saving children and saving the air and water on which we depend. Not all problems in this life will be solved. Some knots are not meant to be untied; they are meant to be enjoyed, to complicate. They are meant to resist unraveling. They are conundra, the ball of it all.

When I speak of the necessity of uncoiling and going from the inside out, I mean walking the labyrinth as a simultaneous spiritual-aesthetic-political act. The walk is political, not because you are compelled to do anything different, but because walking allows time to reflect on one's life, and by the very nature of the reflection to be changed, even if in tiny ways. Walking the labyrinth allows us to change without controlling the outcome of the change. That is why I like it. It combines and links things. Some people actually try to figure out feathers, but why would they? Some people want to tame the mystery of a spider's web. Why? We live in a world where people dissect things. Instead of dissecting things, or dividing them up into little parts for our analysis, those of us who want to love knots can just love them. We can affirm them. Especially in a labyrinth, where linking is the strong message, we can love the knots that others will try to dissect and pull apart. Knots, like everything else, require a point of view. When we shift our point of view from dissection to affirmation, feathers figure themselves out. We are many, many things. It takes a lot to make a feather.

Anyone who has read the children's book *Charlotte's Web* knows that the spider is sure she is creating a magnum opus. Her work was for God's glory, not hers. We could all do the same, especially if we would be sure not to compare our greatness to that of others, our work to other works. When it comes to going back out after we have gone in, often our biggest fear is our own failure. Naming our fear is a good starting place for a labyrinth walk. E. B. White, who wrote *Charlotte's Web*, had this same fear of failure.

For people still spinning a beautiful web, try to make it rare and perfect, not the best. The best is secondary. For choir directors and singers, sing your song, not Heifetz's song. For engineers, build your own building, not someone else's building. Glory is God's; if God wanted all Heifetzes, we would all be Heifetz. Instead, we are who God made us. God spins us on to our magnum opus, one that uses our thread and God's design. When we go into the labyrinth, we go home to our

God and ourselves. When we go out of the labyrinth, we go home to our God and ourselves. One is deeply connected to the other, as are end and beginning.

A tai chi instructor said to a man with a fat belly, "Awesome!" We know what he means. Some things are just amazing; some of those things are us. Life is amazing in large and small ways. When asked about the meaning of creativity, Duke Ellington said there was a soprano saxophonist who could only play a sax in a certain range of six notes. He had tried to get the man to play more, but he wouldn't. He became one of the best members of Ellington's marvelous band because he swore the limitation defined his creativity. Just as the deaf can often see very well, the blind can often hear very well, and the retarded can often love very well, we are sometimes defined by what we do not have. That is awesome! In a world that resists focus, forgiving our dis-ability requires precisely that we focus, that we pay attention to the tragedy of what we do not have, and go on to make beautiful music anyway. It is the very limitations of the labyrinth—a canvas on a floor, some mown grass in a meadow, some rocks placed in circles—that give it its power to let us go in and out simultaneously.

Appendix A

Making Your Own Labyrinth

CAROLE ANN CAMP

DEEPAK CHOPRA SAYS THAT AT ANY MOMENT IN TIME we are faced with infinite possibilities. This saying also applies to designing and creating your own labyrinth. Even though labyrinths fall generally into a few characteristic designs, there is nothing to limit you to these. Once the overall design and shape have been chosen, there are myriad possibilities and choices still to be made. Some people quake at the thought of having so many choices, whereas others revel in the potential creativity before them. There are some questions you need to address before you take pencil to paper, hoe to soil, or paint to canvas.

Where is your labyrinth going to be? Is it going to be in your yard? Is it going to be on a public street? Is it going to be in the city, in the country, or in a town? Is it going to be on public land or private land? Is it going to have easy access or challenging access? Is it going to be at the top of a mountain, in a forest, or on a beach? Is the labyrinth inside or outside? Where do you image your labyrinth?

The answers to some of these questions may depend on whether you are creating your labyrinth alone, with a friend, or with a group. It also depends on whether the labyrinth is for your own private use, for a few people in a designated group, or open to the public. If it is open to the public, will it be open some of the time or all the time?

Another question that needs to be answered early in the decision-making process is: Is this labyrinth going to be permanent or movable?

Once some of these questions have been thought about and maybe answered, the next consideration is size. There are no real rules about the perfect size, although you may want to replicate a labyrinth that already exists, like the one at Chartres, with its numerical symbolism intact. Primarily, however, the size is dependent on use and available space. If you have a small yard, and you are the only one who will ever use it, then a small labyrinth is appropriate. If, however, you plan to have a public labyrinth and you have a large space available, then your labyrinth could be much larger. The size of the labyrinth is also somewhat determined by how many people will be working on its creation and the materials that you will use to make it. For many people, the time actually spent designing and making the labyrinth becomes part of the whole labyrinth experience. However, you may want to consider some time factors in your selection of site and design. If you are drawing a temporary labyrinth on a beach, the process will not be very long or very difficult. If, on the other hand, you want a large labyrinth planted with perennial flowers, it may seem like a daunting task for one person to do alone.

This of course leads to another major question: How is the labyrinth made? This leads to yet another question: What is the path and what separates its parts? If you are painting a labyrinth on a canvas, then the path is painted and the space between the courses (parts of the path) is probably left unpainted, although the opposite of this is also a possibility. If you want a perennial flower labyrinth, then the space between the courses is planted in flowers while the path is just grass that needs to be mowed, or wood chips, or dirt. It is important to think ahead about what the path is made from, and what the spaces between its parts are made from. If you are mowing a grass labyrinth, the mowed grass is the path and the unmown grass is the space between its parts.

When thinking about what your labyrinth is going to be made of, consider also the height of the material between the courses. If you are creating a living labyrinth (e.g., of flowers or shrubs), how high will the plants grow? In Annie's Sunflower Labyrinth in Sunderland, Massachusetts, sunflowers mark the space between the courses. Because the sunflowers are so tall at certain times of the year, one cannot see others walking the path. If you do not want to see others in the labyrinth, choose a border that is tall and thick. If you want to be able to see others, choose plants that are low to the ground, like sweet peas or marigolds. Planted labyrinths pose another consideration. In temperate zones, most flowers bud, bloom, and die. There will be times of the year when the flower path is difficult to discern. The same is true with a grass labyrinth. During the winter months, the path is barely visible. If you live in climates with wide seasonal changes, you may want to have an outdoor summer labyrinth of flowers and an indoor winter labyrinth.

Permanence is another consideration. It is possible to tape a labyrinth to a floor with masking tape. It is possible to set out a rope labyrinth for a weekend retreat. On the other end of this continuum, it is possible to lay a path made of brick or tile, which will withstand wind, weather, and many feet for years to come.

Think about what you want to do and who is going to use this labyrinth. The size of the center circle and the width of the path is determined by what you intend to do once you reach the center and how many people will be included. Read some of the suggested rituals in Part Two. If this labyrinth is solely for your private use, then the center can be small. If you intend to hold many large group rituals, then you will need to make the center bigger.

Once you have decided where the labyrinth is going to be, whether it is going to be permanent or movable, what its maximum size is going to be, whether it will be living or nonliving, what you want to use it for, how many people you want to accommodate at one time, and how many people are going to help create it, you are ready to make a scale drawing of it on paper. This step is very important to the process. Suppose you decide on a seven-course labyrinth with eighteen-inch-wide paths, eight-inch-wide spaces between the courses for perennials, and a center that is ten feet in diameter. You may discover after making a scale drawing that it will not fit in the space you have.

Make a list of the essentials, those things you cannot live without, and a list of those things that can be adjusted or eliminated. For ideas on shapes and styles, see the historical examples in chapter 1; visit labyrinths; find other books on labyrinths in your local library; or visit labyrinth sites on the Internet. Once you have found your ideal labyrinth, draw a picture of it. Most labyrinths are round or rounded, although there have been square ones. Some are perfect circles divided into four basic sections, like the one at Chartres. Some are based on perfect semicircles on the top half and flattened semicircles on the bottom half, similar to the Cretan labyrinth. Cretan-type labyrinths fit more easily into spaces that are not square, allowing the labyrinth to be bigger in one dimension than the other. You can create your own design and shape to fit the space available to you. As you draw your model on paper, be clear in yourself whether the line you are drawing represents the path itself or the space between the paths. It makes a difference how you calculate size: in Figure 1 the lines represent the space between the paths, and in Figure 2 the line represents the path itself (see p. 156).

To lay out your labyrinth on the ground or floor, it is easiest to begin by using a ruler to draw a grid—a pattern of squares—right on your labyrinth drawing. Then determine the size the corresponding grid squares can be on the actual space where the labyrinth will be. When grid size has been determined, re-create the grid—with exactly the same number of squares as the grid on your labyrinth drawing—full size on the ground or on the floor. Then, using your drawing as a guide, you can re-create your labyrinth plan on a large scale by filling in the squares, one by one, based on your drawing. For those who find the grid re-creation method unappealing, I present a simplified method below for laying out a flower labyrinth, using stakes and string.

The Flower Labyrinth

For the purpose of this illustration, let us assume you have chosen the labyrinth in Figure 1. You want to have a living labyrinth with zinnias marking the line between the paths. You want the labyrinth big enough for you and eleven of your friends. You want to be able to gather the group of twelve in the center, and they need to be able to sit down. The center,

FIG. 1

FIG. 2

in this case, has to be at least ten feet in diameter. You have decided on a seven-course path (seven paths on the left, right, and top half of the labyrinth). The width of the path is going to be eighteen inches, and the space in between is going to be eight inches. Remember that you have to maintain the labyrinth after the flowers and weeds start to grow. Plan your path width so that you can easily accommodate a lawnmower or rotary tiller, unless you're paving the path with wood chips or crushed stone. In living labyrinths, weeding is a serious consideration. The length of the path may be determined by how much you like to weed or by how much time you have.

Draw a diagram of the labyrinth you plan to create—either freehand, as in Figures 1 and 2, or using a compass or ruler. Draw horizontal and vertical axis lines through the center of the labyrinth (Figure 3). Use the axis lines to calculate the dimensions horizontally and vertically. In Figure 3 (p. 158), you see sixteen eight-inch spaces between paths, fourteen eighteen-inch paths, and a ten-foot center. Horizontally, this labyrinth is just under thirty-three feet across. Vertically, there are fourteen eight-inch spaces, twelve eighteen-inch paths, and the ten-foot center. Vertically, this labyrinth is close to twenty-eight feet. Use the diagram to determine whether or not the labyrinth will fit the space you have available. At this point in the calculation, you may need to make some adjustments. Hold on to those aspects of the design that are important to you. If you know that there will always be twelve people in the group, making the center circle smaller than ten feet in diameter will make you unhappy later. If, on the other hand, you will be the only one who ever frequents this labyrinth, then a four-foot circle will be big enough.

Once you are completely satisfied with the design, intended uses, and style, and you have worked out all of the calculations, adjusted as necessary, you are ready to begin the actual construction.

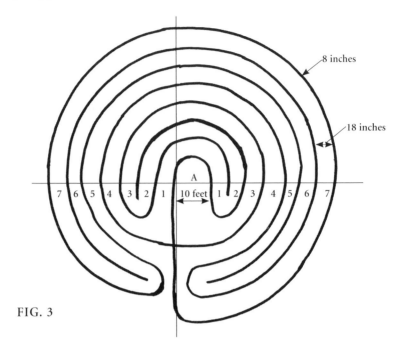

8 inches

18 inches

A

7 6 5 4 3 2 1 | 10 feet | 1 2 3 4 5 6 7

FIG. 3

To mark out your labyrinth on the ground you will need a tall stick, some small sticks, a very long string, some lime or bone meal, and possibly a friend. It is possible to do this by yourself, but a second person really helps. Place the long stick in the ground at what will be the center of your labyrinth, point A in Figure 4. Stake one string across the horizontal (B to C) and one across the vertical (D to E). *Note that the vertical line is not at the center, but tangent to the left side of the center circle.*

For a ten-foot-diameter circle, measure a piece of string five feet long and tie it to the center stick; using it as a compass, mark out the top half of the center circle (Figure 5). It is easier to mark the line with a small stick tied to the end of the string like a pencil and then go back and mark the circumference with bone meal or lime. This is the inside edge of your flower row. Mark the other side of the flower row, in this case eight inches further away from the center than the first circle

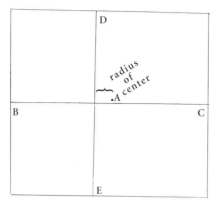

FIG. 4

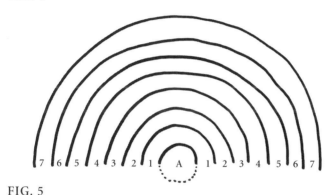

FIG. 5

you drew. An alternative, somewhat simpler way is to draw only one line that will fall in the center of your spacing row or flower bed. Choose one of the methods and make as many semicircles as you need above the center circle, ending at the horizontal string (Figure 5). It will also help to put stakes at both ends of each semicircle, labeling them as in Figure 5.

Starting from the inside and moving to the outside, connect the appropriate lines with corresponding semicircles in the order shown in Figures 6a–6g (pp. 160–163). Two people can complete this process of drawing the labyrinth in about two hours.

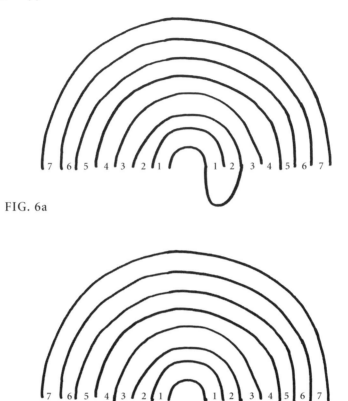

FIG. 6a

FIG. 6b

At this point, timing becomes somewhat of a challenge. It is time to plant. The problem is, if you leave your labyrinth too long between marking and planting, the wind may blow the markings away or the rain may wash them away. Also, if you start from seed, it will take some time for the plants to make themselves known. If you leave your marked labyrinth for some time before planting, at least place many stakes along the lines in case the weather tries to erase your work.

The above method represents one design as an inspiration for others. Whether you chose to paint a labyrinth on a canvas or a street, whether you plan to mow one into your

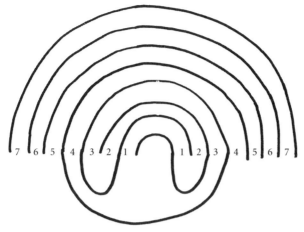

7 6 5 4 3 2 1 1 2 3 4 5 6 7

FIG. 6c

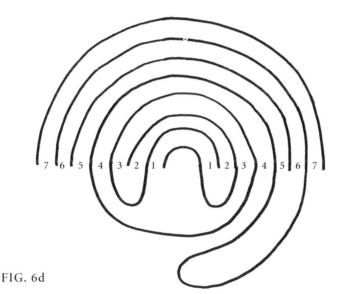

7 6 5 4 3 2 1 1 2 3 4 5 6 7

FIG. 6d

backyard, or whether you plan to create a perennial garden, the process is more or less the same. First create a model on paper—being very clear about whether your line represents the path itself or the space in between. Next calculate the size to make sure it fits where you want it to be. Determine the center. Use a center marker and a long string. Make concentric

FIG. 6e

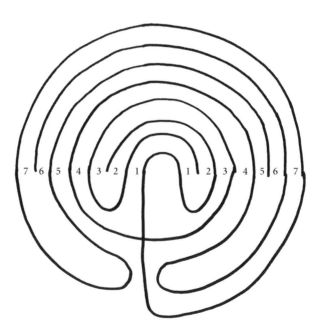

FIG. 6f

FIG. 6g

circles or semicircles. Disconnect the parts of the circles you do not need and connect the ends to make the paths.

There are at least three points in the process where you might want to consider having a blessing ritual for your new labyrinth: when you put in the center pole, when the plants first begin to show above the ground, and when you take your first *real* labyrinth walk.

The very process of making a labyrinth will provide you with much insight and learning. Use the act of creating a labyrinth as a metaphor for how you are creating your life. What do you want your life to be like? Where is your center? What is your compass? What are you putting in the spaces? What are you putting on your path? Whom can you ask to help?

Appendix B

Finding a Labyrinth in Your Area

LABYRINTHS ARE CREATED MORE AND MORE BY A VARI-ety of groups—churches, schools, hospitals, retreat centers, and individuals who want to bring the spiritual and inspirational benefits of the labyrinth walk to the people in their communities. Whether it is a private labyrinth built in a backyard to honor a loved one or one designed by an architect and constructed at a major university to honor the lives lost on September 11, 2001, labyrinths have become a symbol that transcends religious traditions, a spiritual tool for people of all faiths.

In the earlier edition of this book, we listed two or three public labyrinths for each state. Now it is even more impossible to list all the labyrinths available to the public in these few pages. We have selected only a few of the public sites as samples. Each state has many more. If you do not see a labyrinth in your area listed here, there are several websites that will help you in locating one. Or, check with your local church, hospital, or religious retreat center.

> http://labyrinthlocator.com/home
> www.labyrinthenterprises.com/hospitals.html
> www.labyrinthos.net/churchlabuk.html
> www.labyrinthguild.org

ALABAMA

Mental Health Center of Madison County
4040 S. Memorial Pkwy.
Huntsville, AL 35802
(256) 533-1970
www.mhcmc.org

Village Christian Church
700 E. University Dr.
Auburn, AL 36830
(334) 887-5111
www.vccauburn.com

ALASKA

Central Peninsula General Hospital
250 Hospital Pl.
Soldotna, AK 99669
(907) 714-4404

St. Mary's Episcopal Church
2222 E. Tudor Rd.
Anchorage, AK 99507
(907) 563-3341
www.godsview.org

ARIZONA

Franciscan Renewal Center
5802 E. Lincoln Dr.
Scottsdale, AZ 85253

(480) 948-7460
www.thecasa.org

Spirit in the Desert
7415 E. Elbow Bend
Carefree, AZ 85377
(480) 488-5218
www.spiritinthedesert.org

St. Philips in the Hills
4440 N. Campbell Ave.
Tucson, AZ 85718
(520) 299-6421
www.stphilipstucson.org

ARKANSAS

St. Scholastica Monastery
1301 S. Albert Pike Ave.
Fort Smith, AR 72903
(479) 783-4147
www.stscho.org

Washington Regional Medical Center
3215 N. Northills Blvd.
Fayetteville, AR 72703
(479) 463-1000
www.wregional.com/washington-regional-medical-center

CALIFORNIA

Grace Cathedral
1100 California St.
San Francisco, CA 94108
(415) 749-6300
www.gracecathedral.org

Joshua Tree Retreat Center
59700 29 Palms Hwy.
Joshua Tree, CA 92252
(760) 365-8371
www.jtrcc.org

Labyrinth of Life
The Teen Memorial Gardens
Constructed by the Santa Rosa Labyrinth Foundation
425 Morris Ave.
Sebastopol, CA 95472
(707) 545-1656
www.srlabyrinthfoundation.com/sonoma-county-labyrinths/
public-labyrinths-of-sonoma-county-ca/13544540

Unity of Tustin
14402 Prospect Ave.
Tustin, CA 92780
(714) 730-3444
www.unitytustin.org

The Unity Center & Retreat Center
8999 Activity Rd.
San Diego, CA 92126
(858) 689-6500, CA
www.theunitycenter.net

Mercy Center
2300 Adeline Dr.
Burlingame, CA 94010
(650) 340-7474
www.mercy-center.org

Sivananda Yoga Farm
14651 Ballantree Ln.
Grass Valley, CA 95949
(530) 272-9322
www.sivanandayogafarm.org

Center for Spiritual Enlightenment
1146 University Ave.
San Jose, CA 95126
(408) 283-0221
www.csecenter.org

Sunnylands
37977 Bob Hope Dr.
Rancho Mirage, CA 92270
(760) 328-2829
http://sunnylands.org

La Casa de Maria Retreat Center
800 El Bosque Rd.
Montecito, CA 93108
(805) 969-5031
www.lacasademaria.org

COLORADO

Mercy Medical Center
1010 Three Springs Blvd.
Durango, CO 81301
(970) 247-4311
www.mercydurango.org

Penrose-St. Francis Health Services
2222 N. Nevada Ave.
Colorado Springs, CO
(719) 776-5000
www.penrosestfrancis.org

CONNECTICUT

Wisdom House Connecticut Retreat and Conference Center
229 E. Litchfield Rd.
Litchfield, CT 06759
(860) 567-3163
www.wisdomhouse.org

Mercy Center
167 Neck Rd.
Madison, CT 06443
(203) 245-0401
www.mercybythesea.org

Holy Family Passionist Retreat Center
303 Tunxis Rd.
West Hartford, CT 06107
(860) 521-0440
www.holyfamilyretreat.org

DELAWARE
St. Peter's Episcopal Church
211 Mulberry St.
Lewes, DE 19958
(302) 645-8479
www.stpeterslewes.org

Unitarian Universalist Fellowship of Newark
420 Willa Rd.
Newark, DE 19711
(302) 368-2984
www.uufn.org

FLORIDA
St. Luke's Episcopal Church
5150 SE Railway Ave.
Stuart, FL 34997
(772) 286-5455
www.stlukesfl.org

The Episcopal Church of the Good Shepherd
400 Seabrook Rd.
Tequesta, FL 33469
(561) 746-4674
www.goodsheponline.org

GEORGIA
Medical Center of Central Georgia
777 Hemlock St.
Macon, GA 31201
(478) 633-1146
www.mccg.org

Memorial Health University Medical Center
4700 Waters Ave.
Savannah, GA 31404
(912) 350-8000
www.memorialhealth.com

HAWAII

North Hawaii Community Hospital
67-1125 Mamalahoa Hwy.
Waimea, HI 96743
(808) 885-4444
www.nhch.com

Paleaku Gardens Peace Sanctuary
83-5401 Painted Church Rd.
Captain Cook, HI 96704
(808) 328-8084
www.paleaku.com

IDAHO

St. Luke's Regional Medical Center
90 E. Bannock St.
Boise, ID 83712
(208) 381-2222
www.stlukesonline.org/boise

Boise Unitarian Universalist Fellowship
6200 N. Garrett St.
Boise, ID 83714
(208) 658-1710
www.boiseuu.org

ILLINOIS

Central Illinois Natural Health Clinic
1012 W. Fairchild St.
Danville, IL 61832
(217) 443-4372
www.illinoisnaturalhealth.com

Rainbow Hospice
431 N. Claremont Ave.
Chicago, IL 60612
(773) 237-5950
www.rainbowhospice.org

INDIANA

Benedict Inn Retreat Center
1402 Southern Ave.
Beech Grove, IN 46107
(317) 788-7581
www.benedictinn.org

Historic New Harmony
401 N. Arthur St.
New Harmony, IN 47631
(812) 682-4474, (800) 231-2168
www.newharmony.org

Fatima Retreat Center
5353 E. 56th St.
Indianapolis, IN 46226
(317) 545-7681
www.archindy.org/fatima

First United Methodist Church
*Memorial labyrinth for a student who was killed by a car
while jogging*
103 Franklin St.
Valparaiso, IN 46383
(219) 464-0193
www.valpofumc.org/about-us/labyrinth-memorial-garden

IOWA

Prairie Woods
120 E. Boyson Rd.
Hiawatha, IA 52233
(319) 395-6700
www.prairiewoods.org

Collegiate Presbyterian Church
159 Sheldon Ave.
Ames, IA 50014
(515) 292-2063
www.cpcames.org

KANSAS
Trinity Episcopal Church
400 W. Ash Ave.
El Dorado, KS 67042
(316) 321-6606
www.trinityeldorado.org

Grace United Methodist Church
11485 Ridgeview Rd.
Olathe, KS 66061
(913) 859-0111
www.gracech.org

KENTUCKY
Church of the Epiphany
914 Old Harrods Creek Rd.
Louisville, KY 40223
(502) 245-9733
www.churchofepiphany.com

First Christian Church
1106 State St.
Bowling Green, KY 42101
(270) 843-319
www.firstchristianbg.org

LOUISIANA
Hospice of Acadiana
2600 Johnston St. #200
Lafayette, LA 70503
(337) 232-1234
www.hospiceacadiana.com

North Shore Unitarian Universalists
28662 Krentel Rd.
Lacombe, LA 70445
(985) 882-0096
www.northshoreuu.org

MAINE
First Parish Church
9 Cleaveland St.
Brunswick, ME 04011
(207) 729-7331
www.firstparish.net

Trinity Episcopal Church
580 Forest Ave.
Portland, ME 04101
(207) 772-7421
www.trinitychurchportland.org

MARYLAND
Bon Secours Spiritual Center
1525 Marriottsville Rd.
Marriottsville, MD 21104
(410) 442-1320
www.rccbonsecours.com

Johns Hopkins Bayview Medical Center
4940 Eastern Ave.
Baltimore, MD 21224
(410) 550-0100
www.hopkinsbayview.org

MASSACHUSETTS
Boston College
Labyrinth in memory of alumni lost in the 9/11 tragedy
140 Commonwealth Ave.
Chestnut Hill, MA 02467
(617) 552-4700, (800) 669-8430
www.bc.edu/content/bc/alumni/association/labyrinth.html

Rolling Ridge Retreat Center
660 Great Pond Rd.
North Andover, MA 01845
(978) 682-8815
www.rollingridge.org

Kripalu Center for Yoga & Health
57 Interlaken Rd.
Stockbridge, MA 01262
(413) 448-3152
www.kripalu.org

MICHIGAN

Capuchin Retreat Center
62460 Mt. Vernon Rd.
Washington, MI 48094
(248) 651-4826
www.capretreat.org

Weber Retreat Center
1257 E. Siena Heights Dr.
Adrian, MI 49221
(517) 266-4000
http://weber.adriandominicans.org

MINNESOTA

Villa Maria Retreat Center
29847 County 2 Blvd.
Frontenac, MN 55026
(651) 345-4582
www.villamariaretreats.org

Koinonia Retreat Center
7768 Pilger Ave. NW
South Haven, MN 55382
(888) 801-7746
www.koinoniaretreatcenter.org

MISSISSIPPI

Crossgates United Methodist
23 Crossgates Dr.
Brandon, MS 39042
(601) 825-8677
www.crossgatesumcweb.org

Christ the King Lutheran Church
1002 S. Lawndale Dr.
Tupelo, MS 38801
(662) 840-8207
www.christthekingtupelo.com

MISSOURI

Unity Village
1901 NW Blue Pkwy.
Unity Village, MO 64065
(816) 251-3540
www.unityvillage.org

Abbey Road Christian Church
2411 Abbey Rd.
Cape Girardeau, MO 63701
(573) 335-3422
www.abbeyroadchristianchurch.com

MONTANA

Deaconess Hospital
915 Highland Blvd.
Bozeman, MT 59715
(406) 585-5000
www.bozemandeaconess.org

St. Andrew Presbyterian Church
180 24th St.
Billings, MT 59102
(406) 656-9256
http://standrewbillings.org

NEBRASKA

St. Francis Medical Center
2620 W. Faidley Ave.
Grand Island, NE 68801
(308) 395-8272
www.saintfrancisgi.org

Good Samaritan Hospital
10 E. 31st St.
Kearney, NE 68847
(308) 865-7100
www.gshs.org

NEVADA

Carson Tahoe Cancer Center
1535 Medical Pkwy.
Carson City, NV 89703
(775) 445-7500
www.carsontahoecancer.com

St. Rose Dominican Hospitals, San Martín Campus
8280 W. Warm Springs Rd.
Las Vegas, NV 89113
(702) 492-8000
www.strosehospitals.org

NEW HAMPSHIRE

Christ Church Episcopal
43 Pine St.
Exeter, NH 03833
(603) 772-3332
www.christchurchexeter.org

The First Baptist Church of Keene
105 Maple Ave.
Keene, NH 03431
(603) 352-0340
www.firstbaptistkeene.org

NEW JERSEY

Upper Room Spiritual Center
3455 W. Bangs Ave.
Neptune City, NJ 07753
(732) 922-0550
www.theupper-room.org

Hackensack University Medical Center
30 Prospect Ave.
Hackensack, NJ 07601
(551) 996-2000
www.hackensackumc.org

NEW MEXICO

Ghost Ranch Retreat Center
1708 U.S. 84
Abiquiu, NM 87510
(505) 685-4333
www.ghostranch.org

Gila Regional Medical Center, Silver City
1313 E. 32nd St.
Silver City, NM 88061
(575) 538-4000
www.grmc.org

NEW YORK

Bulb Labyrinth Memorial Garden
Memorial labyrinth for children who have lost their lives
Ithaca Children's Garden
615 Willow Ave.
Ithaca, NY 14850
(607) 272-2292
www.ithacachildrensgarden.org/bulb-labyrinth.html

Stony Point Center
17 Cricketown Rd.
Stony Point, NY 10980
(845) 786-5674
www.stonypointcenter.org

Center of Renewal
4421 Lower River Rd.
Stella Niagara, NY 14144
(716) 754-7376
http://center-of-renewal.org

Graymoor Spiritual Life Center
1350 Rt. 9
Garrison, NY 10524
(845) 424-3671, Ext. 2111
www.atonementfriars.org/our_missions_and_ministries/
graymoor_spiritual_life_center.html

Marble Church
1 W. 29th St.
New York City, NY
(212) 686 2770, Ext. 709
www.marblechurch.org

NORTH CAROLINA
Holy Trinity Episcopal Church
607 N. Greene St.
Greensboro, NC 27401
(336) 272-6149
www.holy-trinity.com

Kanuga Conferences
130 Kanuga Chapel Dr.
Hendersonville, NC 28739
(828) 692-9136
www.kanuga.org

NORTH DAKOTA
Christ the King Lutheran Church
713 3rd Ave. N.
Ellendale, ND 58436
(701) 349-3629
pastorgalen@abe.midco.net

St. Stephen's Episcopal Church
120 21st Ave. N.
Fargo, ND 58102
(701) 232-2076
http://ststephensfargo.org

OHIO
Unity Spiritual Center
23855 Detroit Rd.
Cleveland, OH 44145
(440) 835-0400
www.unityspiritualcenter.com

St. Mark's Episcopal Church
1 Trinity Pl.
Toledo, OH 43604
(419) 243-1231
www.trinitytoledo.org

OKLAHOMA
Mercy Health Center
4300 W. Memorial Rd.
Oklahoma City, OK 73120
(405) 755-1515
www.mercy.net/oklahomacityok

Bartlesville Unitarian Universalist Church
428 S. Seneca Ave.
Bartlesville, OK 74003
(918) 336-8385
www.uubville.org

OREGON
Shalom Prayer Center
840 S. Main St.
Mt. Angel, OR 97362
(503) 845-6773
www.benedictine-srs.org/shalom

Sacred Heart Medical Center
1255 Hilyard St.
Eugene, OR 97401
(541) 686-7300
www.peacehealth.org

PENNSYLVANIA
Kirkridge Retreat Center
2495 Fox Gap Rd.
Bangor, PA 18013
(610) 588-1793
www.kirkridge.org

Bethany Retreat Center
1031 Germania Rd.
Frenchville, PA 16836
(814) 263-4855
www.bethanyretreatcenter.org

RHODE ISLAND
Episcopal Conference Center
872 Reservoir Rd.
Pascoag, RI 02859
(401) 568-4055
www.eccri.org

Central Congregational Church
296 Angell St.
Providence, RI 02906
(401) 331-1960
www.centralchurch.us

SOUTH CAROLINA
Mepkin Abbey Retreat Center
1098 Mepkin Abbey Rd.
Moncks Corner, SC 29461
(843) 761-8509
http://mepkinabbey.org

Hospice of the Upstate
1835 Rogers Rd.
Anderson, SC 29621
(864) 224-3358
www.hospicehouse.net

SOUTH DAKOTA
Brookings United Church of Christ
828 Eighth St. S.
Brookings, SD 57006
(605) 697-2882
www.brookingsucc.org

Borderlands Ranch
23120 S. Rochford Rd.
Hill City, SD 57745
(605) 574-4746
www.borderlandsranch.org

TENNESSEE
VA Medical Center
1030 Jefferson Ave.
Memphis, TN 38104
(901) 523-8990
www.memphis.va.gov

Scarritt Bennett Retreat Center
1008 19th Ave. S.
Nashville, TN 37212
(615) 340-7500
www.scarrittbennett.org

TEXAS
Bishop Defalco Retreat Center
2100 N. Spring St.
Amarillo, TX 79107
(806) 383-1811
www.bdrc.org

Kessler Park United Methodist Church
1215 Turner Ave.
Dallas, TX 75208
(214) 942-0098
www.kpumc.org

UTAH

Flanigan's Inn at Zion National Park
428 Zion Park Blvd.
Springdale, UT 84767
(435) 772-3244
www.flanigans.com

Holladay United Church of Christ
2631 E. Murray Holladay Rd.
Holladay, UT 84117
(801) 277-2631
www.holladayucc.org

VERMONT

Hardwick Chiropractic
54 School Cir.
East Hardwick, VT 05836
(802) 472-3033
www.hardwickchiropractic.com

First Universalist Parish of Derby Line
112 Main St.
Derby Line, VT 05830
(802) 873-3563
www.derbylineuu.org

VIRGINIA

Edgar Cayce's Association for Research and Enlightenment
215 67th St.
Virginia Beach, VA 23451
(800) 333-4499, (757) 428-3588
www.edgarcayce.org

Eastern State Hospital
4601 Ironbound Rd.
Williamsburg, VA 23188
(757) 253-5161
www.esh.dbhds.virginia.gov

WASHINGTON
Unity of Bellevue
16330 NE 4th St.
Bellevue, WA 98008
(425) 747-5950
www.unityofbellevue.org

Harmony Hill Retreat Center
7362 E. State Route 106
Union, WA 98592
(360) 898-2363
www.harmonyhill.org

WEST VIRGINIA
St. John's Episcopal Church
1105 Quarrier St.
Charleston, WV 25301
(304) 346-0359
www.stjohnswv.org

RiverWise Park
US-60 & Stonehouse Rd.
Lewisburg, WV 24901
(304) 645-2795
www.dottywood.org

WISCONSIN
Siena Retreat Center
5635 Erie St.
Racine, WI 53402
(262) 639-4100
www.racinedominicans.org/retreats.cfm

Sinsinawa Dominican Center
585 County Rd. Z
Sinsinawa, WI 53824
(608) 748-4411
www.sinsinawa.org

WYOMING
Cheyenne Botanical Gardens
710 South Lions Park Dr.
Cheyenne, WY 82001
(307) 637-6458
www.botanic.org

St. Anthony's Catholic Church
604 S. Center St.
Casper, WY 82601
(307) 266-2666
www.stanthonyscasper.org

International

CANADA
ALBERTA
Faithful Companions of Jesus Christian Life Centre
219 - 19th Ave. SW
Calgary, AB T2S 0C8
(403) 228-4215
www.fcjsisters.ca/fcjcentre

Sisters of Providence
Providence Centre
3005 - 119 St. NW
Edmonton, AB T6J 5R5
(780) 436-7250
www.sistersofprovidence.ca

Centre for Spiritual Living Edmonton
7621 - 101 Ave.
Edmonton, AB T6A 0J6
(780) 469-1909
www.centreforspirit.com

Edmonton Labyrinth Society
11143 - 70 Ave.
Edmonton, AB T6H2G
www.ualberta.ca/~cbidwell/SITES/labindex.htm

BRITISH COLUMBIA

Bethlehem Retreat Centre
2371 Arbot Rd.
Nanaimo, BC V9R 6S9
(877) 889-0517
www.bethlehemretreatcentre.com

Naramata Centre
3375 3rd St.
Naramata, BC V0H 1N0
(877) 996-5751
www.naramatacentre.net

Sorrento Centre
Anglican Church of Canada
1159 Passchendaele Rd.
Sorrento, BC V0E 2W0
www.sorrento-centre.bc.ca/labyrinth.html

University of British Columbia Botanical Garden
6804 SW Marine Dr.
Vancouver, BC V6T 1Z4
(604) 822-3928
www.ubcbotanicalgarden.org

ONTARIO

Galilee Center
398 John St. N.

Arnprior, ON K7S 3H6
613-623-4242
www.galileecentre.com

Ignatius Jesuit Centre of Guelph
Roman Catholic Retreat Centre
5420 Hwy. 6 N.
Guelph, ON N1H 6J2
(519) 824-1250
www.ignatiusguelph.ca

Providence Spirituality Centre
1200 Princess St.
Kingston, ON K7L 4W4
(613) 544-4525
www.spiritualitycentre.ca

The Circle Women's Centre
Brescia University College
1285 Western Rd.
London, ON N6G 1H2
www.thecircle.ca

Mount Carmel Spiritual Centre
7021 Stanley Ave.
Niagara Falls, ON L2G 7B7
(905) 356-4113
www.carmelniagara.com

Five Oaks Retreat Centre
1 Bethel Rd., R.R. #3
Paris, ON N3L 3E3
(519) 442-3212
www.fiveoaks.on.ca

Marguerite Centre
700 Mackay St.
Pembroke, ON K8A 1G6
(613) 732-9925
www.margueritecentre.com

Manresa Jesuit Spiritual Renewal Centre
2325 Liverpool Rd.
Pickering, ON L1X 1V4
(905) 839-2864
www.manresa-canada.ca

Loretto Maryholme Spirituality Centre
379A Bouchier St., Box 1131
Roches Point, ON L0E 1P0
(905) 476-4013
www.lorettomaryholme.ca

St. Peter's Labyrinth at Lourdes Grotto
271 Van Horne St.
Sudbury, ON P3B 1J1
(705) 674-2727
www.grottosudbury.ca

PRINCE EDWARD ISLAND

Healing Presence Christian Retreat
392 Girl Guide Camp Rd., R.R. #2
Murray River, PE C0A 1W0
(902) 962-2023
www.healingpresence.org

SASKATCHEWAN

St. Michael's Retreat Centre
Box 220
Lumsden, SK S0G 3C0
(306) 731-3316
www.stmichaelsretreat.ca

ENGLAND

Church of the Epiphany
227 Beech Ln.
Leeds, LS9 6SW, West Yorkshire
(001) 44 113 2256702
www.epiphanygipton.org.uk

Milton Keynes Council, Campbell Park
1 Saxton Gate
Milton Keynes, MK9 3EJ, Buckinghamshire
(001) 44 1908 233600
www.theparkstrust.com

Saffron Waldon Maze
The Common
Saffron Walden, Essex CB11 1HL
(011) 44 1799 524002
www.visitsaffronwalden.gov.uk

GERMANY

The Labyrinth of 1,000 Women
Traveling memorial for Gertrude Stein, Jane Austen, Jane Goodall, and many others; see website for current location
Schneckenhofstrasse 33
60596 Frankfurt am Main
(011) 49 069 61-25-78
www.frauen-gedenk-labyrinth.de

Berlin Holocaust Memorial Labyrinth
Jüdisches Museum Berlin
Lindenstrasse 9-14
10969 Berlin, Germany
(011) 49 030 259-93-300
www.jmberlin.de

IRELAND

House of Healing
Moneen
Louisburgh, County Mayo
(011) 353 98 66368

Notes

1. Jill Hartwell Geoffrion, *Living the Labyrinth* (Cleveland: Pilgrim Press, 2009).
2. Fredric and Mary Ann Brussat, *Spiritual Literacy: Reading the Sacred in Everyday Life* (New York: Touchstone, 1998).
3. Marilyn Thomas Fulkenberg, *Church, City, and Labyrinth in Bronte, Dickens, Hardy, and Butor* (New York: Lang, 1993), 14.
4. Carolyn Myss, *The Anatomy of the Spirit: The Seven Stages of Power and Healing* (New York: Crown Publishing Group, 1997).

Photo Credits

Page

xii: Congregational Church of San Mateo, San Mateo, California.

vi: Norma Cousins.

16:   Photo by David Weinbler. Courtesy Artistic Pavers, Inc., 300 Big Rock Ave., Plano, Illinois. 60545.

28:   Photo courtesy Barbara Conn, South Deerfield, Massachusetts.

38:   Annie's Garden Center, Sunderland, Massachusetts.

48:   From "A Painting Prayer" medieval labyrinth canvas painting series, photographed by Annette Reynolds.

60:   Prince of Peace Church, Fayetteville, Georgia.

78:   From "Seaside Labyrinth" ©1997 Annette Reynolds, photographed by Melissa Reynolds.

96:   Rev. Jill Kimberly Hartwell Geoffrion.

108:   Kirkridge Retreat Center, Bangor, Pennsylvania.

125:   From "A Painting Prayer" medieval labyrinth canvas painting series, photographed by Annette Reynolds.

126:   Kirkridge Retreat Center, Bangor, Pennsylvania.

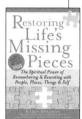
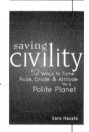
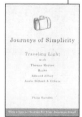

Judaism / Christianity / Islam / Interfaith

All Politics Is Religious: Speaking Faith to the Media, Policy Makers and Community   By Rabbi Dennis S. Ross; Foreword by Rev. Barry W. Lynn
Provides ideas and strategies for expressing a clear, forceful and progressive religious point of view that is all too often overlooked and under-represented in public discourse.   6 x 9, 192 pp, Quality PB, 978-1-59473-374-1 **$18.99**

Religion Gone Astray: What We Found at the Heart of Interfaith
By Pastor Don Mackenzie, Rabbi Ted Falcon and Imam Jamal Rahman
Welcome to the deeper dimensions of interfaith dialogue—exploring that which divides us personally, spiritually and institutionally.
6 x 9, 192 pp, Quality PB, 978-1-59473-317-8 **$16.99**

Getting to the Heart of Interfaith: The Eye-Opening, Hope-Filled Friendship of a Pastor, a Rabbi & an Imam   by Pastor Don Mackenzie, Rabbi Ted Falcon and Imam Jamal Rahman
6 x 9, 192 pp, Quality PB, 978-1-59473-263-8 **$16.99**

Hearing the Call across Traditions: Readings on Faith and Service
Edited by Adam Davis; Foreword by Eboo Patel
6 x 9, 352 pp, Quality PB, 978-1-59473-303-1 **$18.99**; HC, 978-1-59473-264-5 **$29.99**

How to Do Good & Avoid Evil: A Global Ethic from the Sources of Judaism
by Hans Küng and Rabbi Walter Homolka; Translated by Rev. Dr. John Bowden
6 x 9, 224 pp, HC, 978-1-59473-255-3 **$19.99**

Blessed Relief: What Christians Can Learn from Buddhists about Suffering
by Gordon Peerman   6 x 9, 208 pp, Quality PB, 978-1-59473-252-2 **$16.99**

Christians & Jews—Faith to Faith: Tragic History, Promising Present, Fragile Future   by Rabbi James Rudin   6 x 9, 288 pp, HC, 978-1-58023-432-0 **$24.99***

Christians & Jews in Dialogue: Learning in the Presence of the Other   by Mary C. Boys and Sara S. Lee; Foreword by Dorothy C. Bass   6 x 9, 240 pp, Quality PB, 978-1-59473-254-6 **$18.99**

InterActive Faith: The Essential Interreligious Community-Building Handbook
Edited by Rev. Bud Heckman with Rori Picker Neiss; Foreword by Rev. Dirk Ficca
6 x 9, 304 pp, Quality PB, 978-1-59473-273-7 **$16.99**; HC, 978-1-59473-237-9 **$29.99**

The Jewish Approach to God: A Brief Introduction for Christians
by Rabbi Neil Gillman, PhD   5½ x 8½, 192 pp, Quality PB, 978-1-58023-190-9 **$16.95***

The Jewish Approach to Repairing the World (*Tikkun Olam*): A Brief Introduction for Christians   by Rabbi Elliot N. Dorff, PhD, with Rev. Cory Willson
5½ x 8½, 256 pp, Quality PB, 978-1-58023-349-1 **$16.99***

The Jewish Connection to Israel, the Promised Land: A Brief Introduction for Christians   by Rabbi Eugene Korn, PhD   5½ x 8½, 192 pp, Quality PB, 978-1-58023-318-7 **$14.99***

Jewish Holidays: A Brief Introduction for Christians   by Rabbi Kerry M. Olitzky and Rabbi Daniel Judson   5½ x 8½, 176 pp, Quality PB, 978-1-58023-302-6 **$16.99***

Jewish Ritual: A Brief Introduction for Christians
by Rabbi Kerry M. Olitzky and Rabbi Daniel Judson   5½ x 8½, 144 pp, Quality PB, 978-1-58023-210-4 **$14.99***

Jewish Spirituality: A Brief Introduction for Christians   by Rabbi Lawrence Kushner
5½ x 8½, 112 pp, Quality PB, 978-1-58023-150-3 **$12.95***

A Jewish Understanding of the New Testament   by Rabbi Samuel Sandmel;
New preface by Rabbi David Sandmel   5½ x 8½, 368 pp, Quality PB, 978-1-59473-048-1 **$19.99***

Modern Jews Engage the New Testament: Enhancing Jewish Well-Being in a Christian Environment   by Rabbi Michael J. Cook, PhD   6 x 9, 416 pp, HC, 978-1-58023-313-2 **$29.99***

Talking about God: Exploring the Meaning of Religious Life with Kierkegaard, Buber, Tillich and Heschel   by Daniel F. Polish, PhD   6 x 9, 160 pp, Quality PB, 978-1-59473-272-0 **$16.99**

We Jews and Jesus: Exploring Theological Differences for Mutual Understanding
by Rabbi Samuel Sandmel; New preface by Rabbi David Sandmel
6 x 9, 192 pp, Quality PB, 978-1-59473-208-9 **$16.99**

Who Are the *Real* Chosen People? The Meaning of Chosenness in Judaism, Christianity and Islam   by Reuven Firestone, PhD
6 x 9, 176 pp, Quality PB, 978-1-59473-290-4 **$16.99**; HC, 978-1-59473-248-5 **$21.99**

* A book from Jewish Lights, SkyLight Paths' sister imprint

Women's Interest

Women, Spirituality and Transformative Leadership
Where Grace Meets Power
Edited by Kathe Schaaf, Kay Lindahl, Kathleen S. Hurty, PhD, and Reverend Guo Cheen
A dynamic conversation on the power of women's spiritual leadership and its emerging patterns of transformation. 6 x 9, 288 pp, Hardcover, 978-1-59473-313-0 **$24.99**

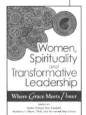
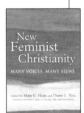

Spiritually Healthy Divorce: Navigating Disruption with Insight & Hope
by Carolyne Call A spiritual map to help you move through the twists and turns of divorce. 6 x 9, 224 pp, Quality PB, 978-1-59473-288-1 **$16.99**

New Feminist Christianity: Many Voices, Many Views
Edited by Mary E. Hunt and Diann L. Neu
Insights from ministers and theologians, activists and leaders, artists and liturgists who are shaping the future. Taken together, their voices offer a starting point for building new models of religious life and worship.
6 x 9, 384 pp, HC, 978-1-59473-285-0 **$24.99**

New Jewish Feminism: Probing the Past, Forging the Future
Edited by Rabbi Elyse Goldstein; Foreword by Anita Diamant
Looks at the growth and accomplishments of Jewish feminism and what they mean for Jewish women today and tomorrow. Features the voices of women from every area of Jewish life, addressing the important issues that concern Jewish women.
6 x 9, 480 pp, Quality PB, 978-1-58023-448-1 **$19.99**; HC, 978-1-58023-359-0 **$24.99***

Bread, Body, Spirit: Finding the Sacred in Food
Edited and with Introductions by Alice Peck 6 x 9, 224 pp, Quality PB, 978-1-59473-242-3 **$19.99**

Dance—The Sacred Art: The Joy of Movement as a Spiritual Practice
by Cynthia Winton-Henry 5½ x 8½, 224 pp, Quality PB, 978-1-59473-268-3 **$16.99**

Daughters of the Desert: Stories of Remarkable Women from Christian, Jewish and Muslim Traditions
by Claire Rudolf Murphy, Meghan Nuttall Sayres, Mary Cronk Farrell, Sarah Conover and Betsy Wharton
5½ x 8½, 192 pp, Illus., Quality PB, 978-1-59473-106-8 **$14.99** Inc. reader's discussion guide

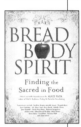

The Divine Feminine in Biblical Wisdom Literature
Selections Annotated & Explained
Translation & Annotation by Rabbi Rami Shapiro; Foreword by Rev. Cynthia Bourgeault, PhD
5½ x 8½, 240 pp, Quality PB, 978-1-59473-109-9 **$16.99**

Divining the Body: Reclaim the Holiness of Your Physical Self
by Jan Phillips 8 x 8, 256 pp, Quality PB, 978-1-59473-080-1 **$18.99**

Honoring Motherhood: Prayers, Ceremonies & Blessings
Edited and with Introductions by Lynn L. Caruso
5 x 7¼, 272 pp, Quality PB, 978-1-58473-384-0 **$9.99**; HC, 978-1-59473-239-3 **$19.99**

Next to Godliness: Finding the Sacred in Housekeeping
Edited by Alice Peck 6 x 9, 224 pp, Quality PB, 978-1-59473-214-0 **$19.99**

ReVisions: Seeing Torah through a Feminist Lens
by Rabbi Elyse Goldstein 5½ x 8½, 224 pp, Quality PB, 978-1-58023-117-6 **$16.95***

The Triumph of Eve & Other Subversive Bible Tales
by Matt Biers-Ariel 5½ x 8½, 192 pp, Quality PB, 978-1-59473-176-1 **$14.99**

White Fire: A Portrait of Women Spiritual Leaders in America
by Malka Drucker; Photos by Gay Block 7 x 10, 320 pp, b/w photos, HC, 978-1-893361-64-5 **$24.95**

Woman Spirit Awakening in Nature: Growing Into the Fullness of Who You Are
by Nancy Barrett Chickerneo, PhD; Foreword by Eileen Fisher
8 x 8, 224 pp, b/w illus., Quality PB, 978-1-59473-250-8 **$16.99**

Women of Color Pray: Voices of Strength, Faith, Healing, Hope and Courage
Edited and with Introductions by Christal M. Jackson
5 x 7¼, 208 pp, Quality PB, 978-1-59473-077-1 **$15.99**

The Women's Torah Commentary: New Insights from Women Rabbis on the 54 Weekly Torah Portions *Edited by Rabbi Elyse Goldstein*
6 x 9, 496 pp, Quality PB, 978-1-58023-370-5 **$19.99**; HC, 978-1-58023-076-6 **$34.95***

* A book from Jewish Lights, SkyLight Paths' sister imprint

Spirituality & Crafts

Beading—The Creative Spirit: Finding Your Sacred Center through the Art of Beadwork *by Rev. Wendy Ellsworth*
Invites you on a spiritual pilgrimage into the kaleidoscope world of glass and color. 7 x 9, 240 pp, 8-page color insert, 40+ b/w photos and 40 diagrams, Quality PB, 978-1-59473-267-6 **$18.99**

Contemplative Crochet: A Hands-On Guide for Interlocking Faith and Craft *by Cindy Crandall-Frazier; Foreword by Linda Skolnik*
Illuminates the spiritual lessons you can learn through crocheting.
7 x 9, 208 pp, b/w photos, Quality PB, 978-1-59473-238-6 **$16.99**

The Knitting Way: A Guide to Spiritual Self-Discovery
by Linda Skolnik and Janice MacDaniels Examines how you can explore and strengthen your spiritual life through knitting.
7 x 9, 240 pp, b/w photos, Quality PB, 978-1-59473-079-5 **$16.99**

The Painting Path: Embodying Spiritual Discovery through Yoga, Brush and Color *by Linda Novick; Foreword by Richard Segalman*
Explores the divine connection you can experience through art.
7 x 9, 208 pp, 8-page color insert, plus b/w photos,
Quality PB, 978-1-59473-226-3 **$18.99**

The Quilting Path: A Guide to Spiritual Discovery through Fabric, Thread and Kabbalah *by Louise Silk*
Explores how to cultivate personal growth through quilt making.
7 x 9, 192 pp, b/w photos and illus., Quality PB, 978-1-59473-206-5 **$16.99**

The Scrapbooking Journey: A Hands-On Guide to Spiritual Discovery
by Cory Richardson-Lauve; Foreword by Stacy Julian Reveals how this craft can become a practice used to deepen and shape your life.
7 x 9, 176 pp, 8-page color insert, plus b/w photos, Quality PB, 978-1-59473-216-4 **$18.99**

The Soulwork of Clay: A Hands-On Approach to Spirituality
by Marjory Zoet Bankson; Photos by Peter Bankson
Takes you through the seven-step process of making clay into a pot, drawing parallels at each stage to the process of spiritual growth.
7 x 9, 192 pp, b/w photos, Quality PB, 978-1-59473-249-2 **$16.99**

Religious Etiquette / Reference

How to Be a Perfect Stranger, 5th Edition: The Essential Religious Etiquette Handbook *Edited by Stuart M. Matlins and Arthur J. Magida*
A straightforward guide to the rituals and celebrations of the major religions and denominations in the United States and Canada from the perspective of an interested guest of any other faith. Covers:
African American Methodist Churches • Assemblies of God • Bahá'í Faith • Baptist • Buddhist • Christian Church (Disciples of Christ) • Christian Science (Church of Christ, Scientist) • Churches of Christ • Episcopalian and Anglican • Hindu • Islam • Jehovah's Witnesses • Jewish • Lutheran • Mennonite/Amish • Methodist • Mormon (Church of Jesus Christ of Latter-day Saints) • Native American/First Nations • Orthodox Churches • Pentecostal Church of God • Presbyterian • Quaker (Religious Society of Friends) • Reformed Church in America/Canada • Roman Catholic • Seventh-day Adventist • Sikh • Unitarian Universalist • United Church of Canada • United Church of Christ
6 x 9, 432 pp, Quality PB, 978-1-59473-294-2 **$19.99**

The Perfect Stranger's Guide to Funerals and Grieving Practices: A Guide to Etiquette in Other People's Religious Ceremonies *Edited by Stuart M. Matlins*
6 x 9, 240 pp, Quality PB, 978-1-893361-20-1 **$16.95**

The Perfect Stranger's Guide to Wedding Ceremonies: A Guide to Etiquette in Other People's Religious Ceremonies *Edited by Stuart M. Matlins*
6 x 9, 208 pp, Quality PB, 978-1-893361-19-5 **$16.95**

Spiritual Practice

Fly-Fishing—The Sacred Art: Casting a Fly as a Spiritual Practice
by Rabbi Eric Eisenkramer and Rev. Michael Attas, MD; Foreword by Chris Wood, CEO,
Trout Unlimited; Preface by Lori Simon, executive director, Casting for Recovery
Shares what fly-fishing can teach you about reflection, awe and wonder; the benefits
of solitude; the blessing of community and the search for the Divine.
5½ x 8½, 160 pp, Quality PB, 978-1-59473-299-7 **$16.99**

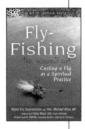

Lectio Divina—The Sacred Art: Transforming Words & Images into
Heart-Centered Prayer *by Christine Valters Paintner, PhD*
Expands the practice of sacred reading beyond scriptural texts and makes it
accessible in contemporary life. 5½ x 8½, 240 pp, Quality PB, 978-1-59473-300-0 **$16.99**

Writing—The Sacred Art: Beyond the Page to Spiritual Practice
By Rami Shapiro and Aaron Shapiro
Push your writing through the trite and the boring to something fresh, something
transformative. Includes over fifty unique, practical exercises.
5½ x 8½, 192 pp, Quality PB, 978-1-59473-372-7 **$16.99**

Dance—The Sacred Art: The Joy of Movement as a Spiritual Practice
by Cynthia Winton-Henry 5½ x 8½, 224 pp, Quality PB, 978-1-59473-268-3 **$16.99**

Everyday Herbs in Spiritual Life: A Guide to Many Practices
by Michael J. Caduto; Foreword by Rosemary Gladstar
7 x 9, 208 pp, 20+ b/w illus., Quality PB, 978-1-59473-174-7 **$16.99**

Giving—The Sacred Art: Creating a Lifestyle of Generosity
by Lauren Tyler Wright 5½ x 8½, 208 pp, Quality PB, 978-1-59473-224-9 **$16.99**

Haiku—The Sacred Art: A Spiritual Practice in Three Lines
by Margaret D. McGee 5½ x 8½, 192 pp, Quality PB, 978-1-59473-269-0 **$16.99**

Hospitality—The Sacred Art: Discovering the Hidden Spiritual Power of Invitation
and Welcome *by Rev. Nanette Sawyer; Foreword by Rev. Dirk Ficca*
5½ x 8½, 208 pp, Quality PB, 978-1-59473-228-7 **$16.99**

Labyrinths from the Outside In: Walking to Spiritual Insight—A Beginner's Guide
by Donna Schaper and Carole Ann Camp
6 x 9, 208 pp, b/w illus. and photos, Quality PB, 978-1-893361-18-8 **$16.95**

Practicing the Sacred Art of Listening: A Guide to Enrich Your Relationships
and Kindle Your Spiritual Life *by Kay Lindahl* 8 x 8, 176 pp, Quality PB, 978-1-893361-85-0 **$16.95**

Recovery—The Sacred Art: The Twelve Steps as Spiritual Practice *by Rami Shapiro;*
Foreword by Joan Borysenko, PhD 5½ x 8½, 240 pp, Quality PB, 978-1-59473-259-1 **$16.99**

Running—The Sacred Art: Preparing to Practice *by Dr. Warren A. Kay; Foreword by*
Kristin Armstrong 5½ x 8½, 160 pp, Quality PB, 978-1-59473-227-0 **$16.99**

The Sacred Art of Chant: Preparing to Practice
by Ana Hernández 5½ x 8½, 192 pp, Quality PB, 978-1-59473-036-8 **$16.99**

The Sacred Art of Fasting: Preparing to Practice
by Thomas Ryan, CSP 5½ x 8½, 192 pp, Quality PB, 978-1-59473-078-8 **$15.99**

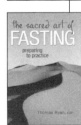

The Sacred Art of Forgiveness: Forgiving Ourselves and Others through God's Grace
by Marcia Ford 8 x 8, 176 pp, Quality PB, 978-1-59473-175-4 **$18.99**

The Sacred Art of Listening: Forty Reflections for Cultivating a Spiritual Practice
by Kay Lindahl; Illus. by Amy Schnapper 8 x 8, 160 pp, b/w illus., Quality PB, 978-1-893361-44-7 **$16.99**

The Sacred Art of Lovingkindness: Preparing to Practice
by Rabbi Rami Shapiro; Foreword by Marcia Ford 5½ x 8½, 176 pp, Quality PB, 978-1-59473-151-8 **$16.99**

Sacred Attention: A Spiritual Practice for Finding God in the Moment
by Margaret D. McGee 6 x 9, 144 pp, Quality PB, 978-1-59473-291-1 **$16.99**

Soul Fire: Accessing Your Creativity
by Thomas Ryan, CSP 6 x 9, 160 pp, Quality PB, 978-1-59473-243-0 **$16.99**

Spiritual Adventures in the Snow: Skiing & Snowboarding as Renewal for Your Soul
by Dr. Marcia McFee and Rev. Karen Foster; Foreword by Paul Arthur
5½ x 8½, 208 pp, Quality PB, 978-1-59473-270-6 **$16.99**

Thanking & Blessing—The Sacred Art: Spiritual Vitality through Gratefulness
by Jay Marshall, PhD; Foreword by Philip Gulley 5½ x 8½, 176 pp, Quality PB, 978-1-59473-231-7 **$16.99**

About SKYLIGHT PATHS Publishing

SkyLight Paths Publishing is creating a place where people of different spiritual traditions come together for challenge and inspiration, a place where we can help each other understand the mystery that lies at the heart of our existence.

Through spirituality, our religious beliefs are increasingly becoming a part of our lives—rather than *apart* from our lives. While many of us may be more interested than ever in spiritual growth, we may be less firmly planted in traditional religion. Yet, we do want to deepen our relationship to the sacred, to learn from our own as well as from other faith traditions, and to practice in new ways.

SkyLight Paths sees both believers and seekers as a community that increasingly transcends traditional boundaries of religion and denomination—people wanting to learn from each other, *walking together, finding the way.*

For your information and convenience, at the back of this book we have provided a list of other SkyLight Paths books you might find interesting and useful. They cover the following subjects:

Buddhism / Zen	Global Spiritual	Monasticism
Catholicism	Perspectives	Mysticism
Children's Books	Gnosticism	Poetry
Christianity	Hinduism /	Prayer
Comparative	Vedanta	Religious Etiquette
Religion	Inspiration	Retirement
Current Events	Islam / Sufism	Spiritual Biography
Earth-Based	Judaism	Spiritual Direction
Spirituality	Kabbalah	Spirituality
Enneagram	Meditation	Women's Interest
	Midrash Fiction	Worship

Or phone, fax, mail or e-mail to: SKYLIGHT PATHS Publishing
Sunset Farm Offices, Route 4 • P.O. Box 237 • Woodstock, Vermont 05091
Tel: (802) 457-4000 • Fax: (802) 457-4004 • www.skylightpaths.com
Credit card orders: (800) 962-4544 (8:30AM–5:30PM EST Monday–Friday)
Generous discounts on quantity orders. SATISFACTION GUARANTEED. Prices subject to change.